RIGHT ON TRACK

OTHER BOOKS BY SANYA RICHARDS-ROSS:

Chasing Grace

Run with Me

RIGHT ON TRACK

RUN, RACE,
BELIEVE

SANYA RICHARDS-ROSS

ZONDERVAN

Right on Track
Copyright © 2018 by Sanya Richards-Ross

This title is also available as a Zondervan ebook.

Requests for information should be addressed to:
Zondervan, *3900 Sparks Dr. SE, Grand Rapids, Michigan 49546*

ISBN 978-0-310-76090-0

Cover design: Brand Navigation
Interior design: Denise Froehlich

Printed in the United States of America

18 19 20 21 22 /LSC/ 10 9 8 7 6 5 4 3 2 1

To My Family,

Most people are fortunate if they have a mother and father in their corner. I've been blessed to have my parents, grandparents, sister, aunts, uncles, and cousins all in complete support of my dreams. There is absolutely nothing I could ever do to repay you all for the sleepless nights, the screams, the encouraging words, the shoulders to cry on, but as a small token I'd love to dedicate *Right on Track* to all of you. Love,

Sanya

CONTENTS

FOREWORD

I started gymnastics when I was six years old. Back then it was pure fun, although I must admit I enjoyed competing too. Even at home, my siblings and I were always playfully trying to outdo one another. The moment I stepped onto the competition floor was both exciting and nerve-wracking. Little did I know then that I would have to learn to master those nerves in order to compete on the world's biggest stage—the Olympics.

After many competitions, falls, obstacles, as well as hard work and some injuries, I finally saw my Olympic dream come into clear focus. But there were times when doubt and fear would creep back in and challenge my mental strength. When you are striving to achieve a goal, mental toughness is such an important skill set to develop. For me, the sport of gymnastics is 80 percent mental and 20 percent physical. As a young athlete, I was looking for techniques that I could relate to and put into practice. I also liked hearing from other athletes. I found they were a wealth of knowledge, experience, and inspiration.

I worked hard and fought for my dreams, and when I emerged from the 2012 London Olympics with two gold medals, my whole life seemed to change overnight. My world felt as if it were flipped upside down! It was such an amazing feeling to accomplish my goals and have the right tools and mindset help make the impossible possible.

I had always been taught to only focus on what I needed to do, but when you are competing, that can sometimes be hard. I remember my coaches always telling me to just think about my routines. When I stepped into the arena and saw all of the Olympic rings, it was hard not to be overcome with nerves, joy, and anticipation. I could see the same was true for all my teammates too. We were all focused on representing the USA to the best of our abilities as well as accomplishing the goals we had individually set for ourselves. At that moment, I also thought about my brother, who had dreams to compete in Track and Field.

We loved watching the races on TV and seeing the men and women literally run after their dreams. I remember cheering for Sanya Richards-Ross during the Olympic Trials, so it would have been awesome if my brother and I could have seen her compete in London. I can't tell you that I followed every single step of her journey to also win a pair of gold medals, but I know that she probably had to face many hurdles and conquer setbacks in order to make it to there too.

She and I also share something else in common. Our spirituality was a powerful force nin helping us cross the "finish line" victoriously! Fast forward a few years later, and it is a pleasure to know Sanya. I consider her a mentor.

Sanya's book would have been helpful when I was growing into my talents and discovering my competitive personality as a young gymnast. It would have been especially nice to have after I made the tough decision to leave my close-knit family at fourteen so that I could take my gymnastics career to another level. It took a huge leap of faith when I moved to Iowa so I could pursue my goal of being the best in the world. Sanya's courageous journey will challenge you to find similar tools that guide you along your path.

When I arrived in West Des Moines, it was cold and full of cornfields. Getting used to a new environment, new gym teammates, and new coaches was challenging. I also had to adjust to living with a host family. The fact that they were so loving and welcomed me as one of their own made the transition easier, but I desperately missed my mom and my siblings. I was thankful for my spiritual upbringing and relied heavily on my faith. The consistent routine of training and schoolwork kept me focused, despite all of the emotions I was feeling.

Hearing about and reading other athletes' stories helped me to see that I was not alone. It doesn't matter if you're ultimately pursuing an Olympic gold medal, striving to graduate with honors, or working to become the best in your profession—we all need structure and discipline in our lives to keep us moving forward.

When you read Sanya's inspirational story of perseverance and resilience, you'll be motivated to keep aiming for success in your own life. I know her book will encourage you to push through during tough times and to focus on achieving your goals.

GABRIELLE DOUGLAS

2012 Women's Artistic Gymnastics All-Around Champion and three-time Olympic gold medalist

INTRODUCTION

T hat's impossible."

A male student in my AP Calculus class was describing his splits—the time on the clock at 400 meters—when running the 800. To improve his personal best, he needed to run 400 meters in less than 51 seconds.

The 400-meter sprint was my event, and I'd already set goals of my own. I'd written them in my journal and placed them on colorful cards taped to the mirror in my bedroom. A pink index card in the top right corner read simply, "50."

"I'm going to run the four hundred in under fifty-one," I announced to my classmate, and the other students who'd begun to listen to our conversation.

"That's impossible," he countered with skepticism.

His arrogance maddened me.

"It's happened before," I reminded him.

We both knew that only one girl, Monique Henderson, had ever run the 400 in less than 51 seconds while in high school in the United States. And we also both knew that she hadn't repeated the time.

"But it's only happened once," he protested. "It was a fluke. Not going to happen again."

"No," I challenged him, energy rising in my voice, "I'm going to do it."

"If you can run it in under fifty-one, I'll give you a hundred dollars."

That was all I needed to hear.

In front of our entire class, we shook on it.

It's been more than a decade since that handshake.

My journey since AP Calculus has taken me to places I never could have dreamed of in high school. With the support of my amazing parents and sister, I've been blessed to pursue my dream of becoming a professional track athlete. I've been given the opportunity to compete against the fastest runners in the world, even winning Olympic gold. I've known God's steadfast love and faithfulness since the day I gave my life to Christ when I was thirteen. And by God's abundant grace, I married the love of my life. If you only looked at the highlights, you'd think my story was charmed.

I want to share with you those headline moments, but I also want to give you a peek at the ones that will never show up on an ESPN highlight reel. In high school, I experienced some deep hurts from people I thought were my friends. At sixteen, I endured a humiliating loss in front of thousands of people I expected to love and support me. In young adulthood, I was diagnosed with a rare disease. Despite my successes, I've faced the same kinds of hurdles that you may be facing today.

And that's why I want to share some of the strategies that have kept me right on track. The lessons I've learned on the asphalt—from my coaches, my teammates, my competitors, and my family—have also taught me what it looks like to run a good race *off* the track. In the work I do today as a communicator and a businesswoman, I am thriving because of all I've been blessed to learn along the way.

But this book isn't just about me. It's about you too! When you decide to run your best race, you can push beyond the limits of what others think you can achieve. When you set your mind to stay on track, you can accomplish amazing things. You may not dream of winning Olympic gold, but perhaps you want to earn a scholarship to college. Maybe you hope to build a strong, healthy family one day. Or perhaps you want to start your own business. With the right strategy, and a commitment to success, I believe that you can accomplish the dreams God has knit into your heart.

The time to start is now. And the place to begin is right where you are. Page by page, I'll teach you how to put one foot in front of the other so you can stay right on track to be the person God created you to be.

I'm cheering for you,
Sanya

P.S. My classmate still owes me $100.

CHAPTER 1

⌒

ON YOUR MARK

S anya, a champion! Sanya, a champion!"
As I walked out of the tunnel into the buzzing arena, I felt overwhelmed by the thunderous applause. The sound of my name being shouted by hundreds of students and parents from my elementary school—Vaz Prep in Kingston, Jamaica—filled my ears and boosted my spirits.

I would not experience the wholehearted devotion of a crowd like that again until competing in the International Olympic Games years later.

Walking toward the starting line, I was wearing new shoes my father had bought me just for this race, and I felt proud to be wearing the school's signature blue-and-gold jersey. The moment was alive with possibility.

Jamaicans are passionate about track and field, and my family was no different. We were just like those crazy screaming fans you've seen on television sporting events. But unlike the growing trend in American youth sports, no one in Jamaica gives out participation ribbons or celebrates a "good try." Winning is everything. Losing is shameful. A second-place finish means only one thing: you were the first loser.

I knew I was fortunate to attend Vaz Prep, a great

17

school that afforded me access to coaches of national caliber. These esteemed coaches had instilled in us the importance of body mechanics at ages as young as six. The school had four houses—yeah, like at Hogwarts in Harry Potter. On the first day of school, each student was assigned to one of those four teams—red, yellow, blue, and green. Random lottery, though; no magic sorting hat. Then, on sports day, students lined up and raced to collect points for their houses. Running for the red team, in second grade, was the first time I remember racing against others. The cheers of students, teachers, and parents were exhilarating. Every stretch, every warm-up drill, every exercise, every practice had prepared me for this moment.

After school, my sister Shari and I would run with our fellow Vaz Prep students on the dirt-and-grass field behind the school. In the absence of a rubber surface, our coaches spray-painted the field with white lines so it resembled a track. Throughout my school day, I sat in class dreaming of the moment after the final bell when my feet would hit the ground and I'd soar around the familiar weedy oval. Eager to feel the wind on my face and body, I'd gather the books I'd need for homework and run out the door to the makeshift track.

This race, though, wasn't being held in the weeds behind the school.

Every year, tens of thousands of people—yes, all those people came to cheer for six-to eleven-year-olds!—filled the National Stadium in Kingston, Jamaica's capital, for a competition called the Prep Champs. The meet determined the country's best youth runners. If you know anything about high school football in Texas—think *Friday Night Lights*—you have a tiny taste of Jamaica's fervent enthusiasm for all things track and field.

My First Race

I was seven years old, and the energy in the stadium for that year's Prep Champs was intoxicating. Fans from Vaz Prep waved blue and yellow flags, pounded their drums, and shouted rehearsed chants.

"Vaz Prep, a champion! Vaz Prep, a champion!"

Because it was my first race competing against other schools, I had no idea how I'd fare against other speedy seven-year-olds. As I squatted down at the starting line for the 60-yard sprint, adrenaline pumped through my frame. I desperately wanted to do my best for my school, for my family, and for myself.

I crouched in anticipation, waiting for the sound of the gun to start the race. Peeking to my right and my left, I checked the competition on either side of me. One girl with long braids looked so nervous.

Should I be nervous? I was so excited, I wasn't sure what emotion to feel.

The other girl, with her hair tied up in a bun, had the confidence of the adult national champions that I already admired, such as Merlene Ottey, Grace Jackson, and Juliet Campbell.

Has she raced before? Is she faster than me?
"On your mark . . ."
I felt a shudder run through my body.
"Get set . . ."
I gulped in a deep breath.
BANG!

The starting gun exploded with a sound that would become the soundtrack for the next several decades of my life.

Legs pumping, holding my head and arms and back in the posture my coaches had taught me, I pushed to the front of the pack. Running as hard as my skinny-girl legs would carry me, I pulled ahead of the other runners after about twenty meters, and held my lead until I dipped across the finish line.

I'd won!

Finding Your Thing

I was lucky to discover what I was most passionate about when I was young. I think that's pretty rare, though. More often, young people haven't yet identified their passion.

Maybe that's you.

Maybe you've noticed that boy who's been playing ice hockey since he was three, or the girl who's been raising money for orphans since she was six, and you feel like you're already behind if you haven't found your own "thing."

I've got good news for you: you're actually normal. Don't worry if you don't yet know what you like, or where you excel.

The best way to find your passion is to experiment.

When I was ten, I joined our school's netball team. It's kind of like basketball, without the dribbling. You can watch it on YouTube—it's a great game. Although netball didn't turn out to be my driving passion, I learned strategy and teamwork, and I strengthened my body by playing it. I gave it my everything and progressed all the way to representing Jamaica on the national junior netball team.

Now if my skill sets would have carried over to basketball, I might have become the next WNBA superstar like Lisa Leslie. When my family immigrated and I tried out for basketball, I quickly realized just how different the two games were. In netball, you're not allowed to dribble and the hoop has no backboard. Yes, I could jump, catch, and run, but never learning to dribble meant it was really hard to make the transition. I stuck with basketball for a few years—I loved being a part of a team—but ultimately decided to focus on track and field after my sophomore season.

Netball wasn't all I tried.

My sister Shari was a great dancer, so I joined her in trying out for our school's dance team. The team danced in modern and traditional African dance, as well as a Jamaican style of reggae dance hall. I made the team, but I was certainly not the shining star dazzling audiences with my dance solos. I was okay, but I wasn't great. We practiced every day, and at the end of the year the team performed for our school and for our parents. We had cool, colorful costumes, and I loved spending time with Shari and being a part of the close-knit group.

Here's the thing: I could have just stuck with running. I didn't really need to prove to everyone that I was the second-to-worst dancer on the dance team. But I'm so glad I gave it a shot. I grew because I exercised the courage to try something new, and—even though I wouldn't dance professionally—that experience built my confidence in myself and my ability to try new things.

And although my first 60-yard sprint is now a warm, distant memory, I actually had to *try* running before I knew it would be my driving passion.

Before I ever ran my first lap around Vaz Prep's makeshift track, I understood how important running was in Jamaica. The capital shut down during the Olympics—and I don't mean because Jamaica was the host country, because it never has been. Our enthusiasm for track and field was just so great that, no matter where the Olympics were being held in the world, our nation hit Pause during the event. Before I ever laced up my running cleats, I knew I wanted to be like the champions my family watched as a young girl.

But guess what? I still had to try it.

I had to show up to the first day of practice after school and learn to do warm-ups.

I had to run my first race against kids in my grade.

I had to show up. Feel awkward. Learn the sport. Try my best.

If I hadn't—because of fear, or insecurity, or because I believed the boys who said that girls could never beat boys—I would have missed out on the great joy of living out my purpose by doing the thing that God created me to do.

If I hadn't shown up and given it a try, I never would have discovered that I could beat those boys who'd taunted me.

What Will You Try?

When I speak to students, I hear a lot of them say things like:

"I don't know what I like."

"I'm not that good at anything."

"I haven't found my passion."

I get that. And if that's how you feel, know that you're in good company.

You may feel that other students have landed on the thing they're passionate about: history or math or sewing or skating or running.

Whichever group you find yourself in today, I want to encourage you to keep trying new things.

The path to finding your passion and living your dreams is in trying new things.

Try out for the school speech team and stand in front of an audience and judges to perform your own original monologues. You may find you have something important to say.

Get an after-school job—babysitting, or waitressing, or working retail—where you can earn money and gain job experience for whatever your next, better job might be.

Start a lawn business—mowing, or raking, or shoveling sidewalks—to see if you have an aptitude for marketing a business.

Take a pottery class.

Compose a song.

Build a website.

You don't have to land on your ultimate passion the first time you try something new. Chances are that you won't! But no matter what you try, you'll be gathering tools and skills that will help you once your particular passion becomes more clear. I guarantee that you'll be stepping in the right direction each time you experiment by trying something new.

My sister Shari is a great example. I told you she was a great dancer. (She still is!) But when we were young, she was also interested in doing other girls' hair. I had some of the coolest hairdos in high school—sew-in extensions for prom, microbraids for track meets, and cornrows for day to day—because Shari was experimenting with her passion for hair when we were young. If Shari had decided she was only going to dance, and had refused to try anything else, both of our lives would be so different now! Today we own a salon together, and I get to see Shari thriving daily as she shares her unique purpose with the world.

But she never would have discovered it if she had not also tried a host of other things.

My husband, Ross, is another great example. He didn't play football for his high school until his sophomore year. Sophomore year! In a state where most boys start playing football at seven. He went on to play football at the University of Texas, winning the Jim Thorpe Award as the nation's top defensive back. He also played for the New York Giants in two Super Bowls, including in 2007 when the Giants beat the then-undefeated New England Patriots!

But what if Ross hadn't shown up for summer conditioning before his sophomore year of high school? What if he'd just bowed out because he assumed that other guys, who'd been playing longer, would beat him? My swift, strong, smart, faithful husband would not have lived out his purpose had he not tried something new when he was sixteen years old.

What new thing has your name on it today?

Live Courageously

Your purpose begins with trying something new, and trying something new begins with courage. It requires being brave.

But what if I could guarantee you that, if you tried something new, you couldn't fail?

I can.

I guarantee that each thing you try—such as taking a cooking class, learning calligraphy, or serving older folks at a nursing home—is a guaranteed win, because that experience, whether a seeming failure or an obvious success, equips you with new tools. You might learn what *not* to do in the kitchen by forgetting to put yeast in the bread dough. You might learn how to get India ink out of the carpet following a calligraphy mishap. Or if you struggle to form relationships with older folks in the nursing home, that experience might move you one step closer to realizing you love caring for toddlers.

You can't fail when you try something new because—even

if your attempt seems like a fail—you've grown from what you've learned.

So, yeah, that was kind of a trick question.

But what I want you to hear is that the path to discovering your passion and living out your dreams begins with trying new things. And if marching band, or salsa class, or chess club don't work out, you've still *won* because you've learned something about yourself and are one step closer to discovering what you're meant for.

In my journey, everything I gained from netball and calculus and dance team and journaling has made me a richer person with a broader range of skills and interests that I can enjoy myself as well as offer the world. For instance, when I was sixteen I never would have guessed that I'd be writing a book. Yet as I open the journals I've kept for years, I'm finding all the little breadcrumbs that led me to where I am today.

So, for now, it's okay not to know where you'll land. If you can't yet see the gold medal podium, or the Oscar statue, or the Oval Office, that's all right.

The path to finding your passion is trying new things.

My Thing

The first time I raced in Kingston's massive National Stadium, I had no way of knowing where those first adrenaline-fueled steps on my skinny legs would take me.

But, while gulping in air at the end of my race as I paced several more meters down the track, I glanced up into the crowded stands to see my mom and dad cheering wildly for me. Grinning, I waved at them, and walked to the edge of the arena to find my warm-up clothes.

As I was gathering my things, my mom and dad ran down onto the field. My dad scooped me up in his arms and they both hugged me. Each of them beamed with pride.

At the end of the meet, I stood on the highest step of the podium and was named the fastest seven-year-old girl in the region. I beamed with joy as the tall official draped a gold medallion over my head.

I loved feeling the heavy weight of the medallion around my neck.

I wanted to feel it again.

RIGHT ON TRACK CHALLENGE

Do you feel like you've discovered your thing? Have you found what gives you a sense of purpose in life?

- What is something that brings you satisfaction?
- What gives you great joy?
- What could you do for hours without ever looking at the clock?
- What do you do that nourishes you and fills your tank?
- What blesses others as it blesses you?

Make a list of the activities you enjoy and offer them to God. Ask God to show you what you've been uniquely designed to do.

CHAPTER 2

SETBACKS

B y the time I was in third grade, I'd gotten a little cocky. Because I had done so well at the Prep Champs as a seven-and eight-year-old, and because I continued to win races, I'd developed a reputation in Jamaica. By the time I was nine, I was known as one of the fastest young athletes in the country. Race fans couldn't wait to see me run.

I competed in my third Prep Champs when I was nine.

Even though elementary school runners didn't use starting blocks the way the high school athletes did, our coach was training our bodies to learn the starting position we would use a few years later. We emulated the posture and stance of runners using the blocks, but that meant it was possible to lose our balance if we misjudged the stance.

For my 60-yard dash, I was slotted in lane 4, beside my biggest rival.

Vaz Prep had an ongoing rivalry with Wolmer's Prep School. Both produced outstanding runners, and every year the competition got pretty intense. When two schools are that good, the trash talk gets fierce. The schools would even sit side by side in the stands and shout wildly for victory.

"Our girl's gonna win!" Wolmer's yelled. "You got this, Vanessa!"

Vanessa Williams was my most challenging competitor. And she also used the same starting position we'd been taught at Vaz.

The announcer began the familiar liturgy: "Stand tall . . ."

We each took a deep breath.

"On your mark . . ." We relaxed our bodies.

When he chimed, "Get set . . .", we each dropped down into a three-point stance, almost like a quarterback.

Vanessa and I crouched down as if we were in the blocks, steadying ourselves with one hand on the ground. Without the stability of the blocks underfoot, the pose required stillness and careful balance.

Seconds felt like hours, waiting for the signal to run.

BANG!

The gun exploded to start the race.

Maybe I was too sure of myself. Maybe my focus was compromised. Whatever the reason, I lost my balance and rocked in reverse when the gun fired. I tumbled backward on my hands and Vanessa was *gone*.

It was my first moment, though certainly not my last, of complete panic.

In the split second of that stumble, a single thought filled my mind: *I'm the fastest girl, and if I lose this race I won't be the fastest girl.*

I don't know how to explain the weight and meaning of

that moment. I think that I could have handled a loss *personally*, but the meaning of that race was bigger than me. I wasn't just running for myself. I was running for my school. I was running for my family. And for the first time, I realized I was running to meet other people's expectations.

Still startled by the fumble, but driven to remain the fastest girl, I hopped up and started running swifter than I'd ever run before. Though there's no simple formula to calculate how fast I would have had to run to recover from my fall, pass the other competitors, and eventually catch Vanessa, the unlikely odds are what have me convinced that it could be the fastest I'd ever run before going pro. With just ten meters between the finish line and whoever would reign as the fastest girl, I eked past Vanessa to cross the finish line one stride ahead of her.

Having lost my cocky edge, aware of how close I'd been to defeat, I was thrilled and relieved to have won.

As you might guess, the fans in Vaz Prep's section of the stands lost their minds. They went absolutely wild.

Rough Starts

What I learned that day has taught me as much about life as it has about running: sometimes you don't get off to a perfect start.

I'm thinking of young people who didn't come from the kind of secure, loving home that I had the privilege of enjoying. I'm thinking of kids, in the United States and around the globe, who are born into poverty. I'm thinking of those born with physical or intellectual disabilities. There's no rulebook that says that everyone gets an equal start in life.

We don't.

If not at the very beginning of your life, you may have faced obstacles a little later on. Maybe you didn't have two loving parents in your home. Maybe you had to leave your friends and move to a new city. Maybe you thought you were running the 100-meter sprint, and halfway down the track you realized someone had put a hurdle in your lane you never expected: an illness, a death, a divorce, an injury. I want you to hear that no matter what kind of start you get, or what might throw you off along the way, you can still finish strong and live out the good purpose God has for your life.

If you're wired like me, you might think that hopping up and scrambling to run for my life was the only choice I could have made. It wasn't. Over the years I've spent on the track, I've seen athletes in similar situations who didn't give their best performances when faced with a challenge. Some who've had a rough start have chosen to bail out completely. I've seen others fake an injury rather than completing the race with dignity when all eyes were on them. I think that weird moment when I was nine taught me not to give up, even if it meant not winning. It set the tone for my career and my life.

As you think about the obstacles you may have faced already, I hope that you can close your eyes and see yourself powering beyond them and finishing your race with grace, dignity, and power. If you pick yourself up and give it everything you have, even if you're not the first one to cross the finish line, you can be as proud of that finish as someone else might be of winning gold.

I was when it happened to me years later.

The Final Finish

I'm going to give you a sneak peek at the conclusion of my racing career, because in some ways it mirrored my race as a nine-year-old, even though it didn't end on the awards podium.

During the last six or seven years of my running career, the big toe on my right foot began to suffer compound injuries. When a 2012 surgery failed to improve my function or comfort level, and left two screws in my toe, I continued to suffer daily agony. Then an airline passenger stepped on that toe in 2015, crushing one of the screws, and the pain became excruciating. The requisite surgery cost me four months of training for the 2016 Olympic trials. When I was finally authorized to run, after a hamstring injury compounded my setbacks, I needed at least four to six weeks to prepare for the Olympic trials.

I had three.

Anticipating the trials, I was really excited about running on a track that was close to my heart, Hayward Field in Eugene, Oregon—and nothing was going to keep me from it. I knew deep inside that I wasn't likely to make it, because I just wasn't healthy enough, but I still had to try. If God wanted me in Rio, I'd go to Rio.

I lined up at the starting blocks beside women I knew and respected: DeeDee Trotter, Francena McCorory, and

Natasha Hastings. In this entirely counterintuitive situation, where you have to beat your American teammates in order to run together for America, we wished each other well. And we meant it.

The moment I left the blocks, I had a feeling something was off. Then, halfway through the race, I pulled up. Even though the other runners were beyond my reach, a more mature version of my inner nine-year-old, one who no longer needed to perform to please others, finished that race.

As I continued around the track, I heard a woman yell from the bleachers, "We love you, Sanya!"

There was a day when the proud Jamaican in me would have shrugged off her support. A little voice would have whispered in my ear, "Second place is the first loser." But in that moment, I was able to receive her care and the cheers of so many others in the stands.

But because I'd already envisioned myself winning in Rio, it was a bittersweet moment.

I jogged to the finish line, where I received a standing ovation from the crowd of avid American track and field enthusiasts. I heard hundreds of people shouting out how much they loved me.

Though I wouldn't have chosen to face the obstacles that prevented me from competing in Rio, I am proud that, ultimately, they didn't win.

If the obstacles had won, I would have seen the end of my running career as a failure, rather than the gateway to the new opportunities I've been able to embrace.

Don't Quit

I want you to hear that setbacks—whether literal, like mine, or figurative—do not have to sink you. If you've faced unique challenges that your friends or other people your age haven't faced, you've been given opportunities to dig deeper and fight harder. Life will never be perfect, but the obstacles you face don't have to hinder you from success. In fact, if you allow them, the obstacles will propel you forward to greatness.

When I was nine, a setback propelled me to victory on the track.

When I was twenty-nine, a setback propelled me to success off the track.

I know a young woman who'd just completed her track career at Norfolk University when she was involved in a horrific train accident. April was twenty-eight when she lost her leg. She had a good job and had just bought her first home. It was one of those unexpected, life-altering moments that no one anticipates. While she was still in the hospital being fitted with a prosthetic leg, April read about the Paralympics and was motivated to make her comeback to the track. In 2004, April Holmes competed and medaled in her first Paralympic games, and went on to win gold in the 2008 Paralympic Games in the 100-meter sprint.

What anyone would view as a setback, and what some would view as an insurmountable obstacle, didn't keep her from running her race.

Your challenge might not be physical. Maybe you have

to work really hard in school to get Cs and Bs. You may have to put more energy than most into making friends. Or maybe there are challenges within the family you were born into—disease or addiction or mental illness. The setbacks and obstacles you face don't determine how fast or how far you'll go in life. I believe that, in the face of any hardship, you have the courage within you to pick yourself up and run your own race.

The win is in getting back up again, no matter how many times you get knocked down.

RIGHT ON TRACK CHALLENGE

Consider the setbacks you have faced and are facing:

- What obstacles were caused by others?
- What challenges were unavoidable?
- What setbacks were a result of your choices?
- What roadblocks have you already overcome?

Setbacks are unavoidable. Notice the strength you've already demonstrated and ask God to help you with the additional obstacles, challenges, and roadblocks you'll face in the future.

CHAPTER 3

TAKE LIFE IN STRIDE

The evening our parents told Shari and me that we would be moving from Jamaica to Miami, Florida, we *begged* them not to make us move. I was in my last year of elementary school and had been looking forward to starting middle school. I didn't want to leave my friends, my team, my school, and my coaches.

My mom had already landed a job in Florida by the time they talked to us. My parents saw opportunities were available in the United States that weren't available in Jamaica.

"No, you move," I bargained. "We'll stay here. We can stay with Aunt Bev. We'll be fine!"

There was one problem: My parents weren't moving to score opportunities for themselves. They wanted to relocate so that Shari and I would have the chance to earn scholarships and attend great universities. My aunt Maureen, in Florida, and aunt Claire, in Maryland, had convinced our parents that we needed to move to access those opportunities. Their children, who were around my age, had already been living in the States for several years, and they wanted us to join them. The longer we waited, they warned, the less likely we'd be to earn scholarships.

"Please, please, please, please, let us stay here," Shari begged.

"We promise," I negotiated, "that we'll do well in school, and we can still attend college in the United States."

Our parents weren't going for it.

"But I just got into Immaculate Conception!" I whined.

The education system is a bit different in Jamaica. Everyone takes a common entrance exam, and your scores determine what schools you attend. Immaculate Conception was one of the best school for girls, and the hardest to get into, but I'd gained admission! My parents had been so proud of me too. They knew it was a great school, but they still weren't budging.

When Shari and I saw their resolve, we bargained to finish out the last three months of the school year in Jamaica. After some private conversations, my parents agreed. They arranged for Shari and me to stay with the principal of Vaz Prep, who was a good friend of my mom's. My parents moved to a city near Miami called Pembroke Pines, Florida, where they were having a house built, so my mom could start her job while Shari and I finished up the school year. We were probably happier about going to school than any of the other kids! With the June move to America looming, every day felt precious.

Moving from Jamaica to the United States was much different than moving between two American cities. Sure, we would miss our friends like anyone would. But Jamaica was a small island, and we knew a lot of the people on it! We'd be leaving the music we loved, the culture, and a tight-knit beach community where we were known and loved. Where else but in track-loving Jamaica would everyone on the island know one eleven-year-old girl who happened to be a fast runner?

We were leaving a warm, cozy nest for the bustle of a big new city where we knew almost no one.

Welcomed

Thankfully, when we arrived in Pembroke Pines in the middle of June, our older cousins Kevin and Shelley, who were fifteen and nineteen years old, were there to welcome us. Because they'd moved from Jamaica to the U.S. when they were young, they were more American than Jamaican.

Shelley coached me, "Just be nice to people. Be respectful. You'll do great."

Kevin tried to assure me everything would be fine, promising, "You're funny, and you're sweet. Just be yourself."

That was the best advice I received.

Facing change can be scary. Whether it's change we choose, like stepping up to take an honors class, or change that's chosen for us, like moving to another country, there will always be adjustments we need to make.

Change is hard.

And as we're adjusting, we want to be accepted by others. We might think that if we look right, dress right, speak right, or act right, then others will welcome us with open arms. Whether we're young or old, it can be very tempting to be who we're not in order to fit in. Without ever meaning to, we start becoming like the people around us.

I think there are two main reasons we're tempted to act like others as we're adjusting to change.

The first is so that we don't stick out. We don't want to draw attention by wearing the wrong clothes. We don't want to be seen without a cohort of friends. We don't want to be caught without the latest phone or gadget.

The second reason we can be tempted to be like others as we're adjusting to change is because we *do* want to stick out! We want to be recognized the way others have been. It's why an athlete might imitate the technique or strategy she's seen another athlete use to succeed. It's why a writer might pick up the voice of a writer she admires. Or why a musician might imitate the sound of a popular performer. In the end, though, trying to be like someone else will leave you exhausted and lonely, because you never get to become *who you are*.

As you face change and adjust to new circumstances, you will thrive if you can stay true to who you are.

Be You

"Have fun," my cousin Kevin had encouraged me. "Just be yourself."

His words continued to echo in my ears over the summer as our family adjusted to life in America, and even more so as school began.

In Jamaica, we'd always worn uniforms to school. On my first day of sixth grade in Florida, I got to *choose* what I wore to school. I basically freaked out about it, planning for an entire week before classes began. I tried on everything in my closet before finally settling on a denim dress with white Chuck Taylors.

I admit it, I wanted to fit in *and* stand out!

I walked into my first-period class and scanned the room to choose a desk to sit in. Most of the seats were taken. The kids who wanted some distance from the teacher had filled in the back rows, and the kids who wanted to capture the teacher's attention were filing into the front rows. I sat down at a desk in the middle of the room and opened my binder as if I had something really meaningful to do in there. Kids who hadn't seen each other all summer were catching up with one another when the teacher walked in.

Instinctively, I leapt to my feet.

In Jamaica, it was common practice for the entire class to stand as a sign of respect when the teacher entered the classroom. When twenty-seven pairs of eyes looked at me standing at attention in the middle of the classroom, like some Martian soldier who'd just landed from outer space, I quickly realized this was not standard protocol in American classrooms and slunk back down into my seat.

Starting middle school in a *new country* meant a lot of adjustments!

When I told Shari about it at lunch, thinking she'd probably also stood when the teacher walked in, she burst out laughing at me. Apparently, she'd had the good sense to read the room and figure out that the other students were staying seated.

Great first day, right?

But throughout those first few months, I kept hearing Kevin's words: "Just be yourself."

Find Your Groove

A few months after school started, I saw signs up around the school advertising tryouts for the girls' basketball team. Although I didn't know it at the time, trying out for basketball was probably one of the best moves I could have made. It was an easy way to build relationships with new friends. All the girls on the team loved sports, and working together was a natural way to bond.

I know that athletic competition isn't for everyone, but if you are open to trying it out, I encourage you to do so. Yes, it's a great place to make friends. But there's so much more value in sports that ripples through other areas of your life.

Sadly, research has shown that a lot of girls try sports, but then drop out between the ages of eleven and fourteen. Back when my mom was a girl in the 1960s, there was this myth that sports were for tomboys. Even today, as some girls move into puberty and become more interested in their appearance and in boys, they might decide that athletic competition isn't for feminine girls.

Nothing could be farther from the truth.

In fact, I'm proud to say that I'm one of the most feminine girlie girls I know. I love getting my nails and hair done, and dressing to look my best. And I'm not the only one; if you've seen any of the last few Olympics, check out the hair and nails on the track athletes. For some races, the starting blocks look like a beauty pageant! The old myth that sports are for boys, or for tomboys, just isn't true.

Unfortunately, a number of girls today take the opportunities available to female athletes for granted. It's important to know, though, that as recently as the 1960s and early 1970s, girls and women were denied many opportunities to compete at sports that were available to their male peers. That all changed with Title IX, a 1972 Educational Amendment guaranteeing that people can't be excluded based on their sex from participation in educational programs or activities that receive federal financial assistance. We are incredibly fortunate today that so many possibilities are available.

I've learned many things through sports that have developed who I am as a person off the track, court, and field. I've gained confidence that I'm a capable person who can do anything I set my mind to. I'm more fearless, because I know what I'm able to accomplish. So much of what I learned through sports translates into what I'm doing every day in business, media, communications, and even marriage!

Consider sports. And don't believe that just because some girls might have been playing soccer since they were three, or basketball since they were eight, that you're behind. Remember, my husband, Ross, started football in tenth grade. If you want to try out for your school's tennis team, or if you want to get some great exercise by joining the swim team, go for it. Sports can help you grow and develop into the kind of resilient person who's adept at navigating change.

Something New

As you face new or changing circumstances in your own life, I hope you'll gather your courage to try something new, even if it's not sports.

Maybe you'll find your groove by joining the chess club or a foreign language club. Or maybe you'll explore the theater or even join an art class. Trying out a host of opportunities gives you the chance to discover what you're good at and what brings you joy.

I'd also encourage you to keep your eyes open for opportunities to serve others. Our society bombards us with the message that our lives should be all about us and the next flattering selfie we can post on social media. But Jesus calls us to something radically different when he invites us to spend our lives serving others. Maybe you know of a nursing home where lonely folks would welcome a visit. Or maybe there's a student at school with an intellectual disability who'd love to go to a movie with you. If you keep your eyes open, God will show you the people he loves whom you can love too. Though it seems counterintuitive, when you're facing changes and challenges in your own life, helping others helps you.

A final reason it's great to explore new possibilities is that the place where you find meaning and fulfillment is also where you can connect with people who love what you love. One of the reasons that basketball and track were such a win for me in my new school was that they also provided a great sense of community. My teammates and I clicked because of what we shared in common. Those friendships became a safe space where I could be myself. Even if you have a good group of friends, stay open to the possibility that there might be someone new who can be a supportive friend.

Adapt and Grow

As you face new circumstances—new schools, new friends, new challenges—you'll probably start out feeling uncomfortable and gradually grow more comfortable. That's normal. And while comfort is great, I want you to consider the possibility that God might have even more for you.

For instance, one of the first friends I made at Pines Middle School was Karel Crawford. We clicked right away. Karel had four or five close friends, so we all ate lunch together. Through Karel, I ended up developing friendships with those other girls. As a new student, it felt great to be welcomed and accepted by them.

After a bit, I began to branch out. In fact, I loved moving around and sitting with all different kinds of students. As I got more and more comfortable being in my own skin—in Kevin's words, just *being myself*—everyone in school was fair game to be my friend! So while it was great to be welcomed by others, I eventually became the *welcomer*. I didn't stay in my comfort zone, but began to reach out to get to know other people.

If you're an introvert, I know that probably sounds horrible. But even introverts can welcome one new person who's facing adjustments of their own.

Sometimes we choose changes and other times they choose us. It's natural to have some anxiety about facing and adapting to new circumstances. As you decide to be flexible—and be yourself!—I'm confident that you can take change in stride.

RIGHT ON TRACK CHALLENGE

What kinds of change have you faced or are facing now?

- Have you moved between houses, cities, states, or countries?
- Have you lost a loved one?
- Has your family changed because of divorce or other loss?
- Have you faced health challenges?
- Have you navigated other tricky changes?

Throughout your life, you'll face a variety of changes. What resources will you use to take them in stride?

CHAPTER 4

BE TRUE TO YOU

On my first day of sixth grade in Florida, wearing my denim dress and white Chuck Taylors, I had butterflies in my stomach as my dad dropped Shari and me at the curb of Pines Middle School.

Would I be accepted? Would I have friends? Would I fit in?

I'm pleased to report that, in my first-period class, one of the girls complimented me on my shoes.

Thank you, God.

There were a lot of differences between life in Jamaica and life in America. In Jamaica, we're proud of our flavorful cuisine. At my school, we'd have warm, cooked meals at lunch that included Jamaican rice, chicken, and vegetables. At my new school, though, I was surprised to be served cold chocolate pudding, pizza, and French fries. Because my diet was so important in our home, I knew I'd be bringing my own lunch to school.

Students' attitudes toward adults were also different. In the school I'd attended, teachers wielded a lot of authority. We respected them the way we would a parent or an aunt or uncle. If a student gave a teacher attitude, or talked back, he could be sent to the principal's office for a spanking! In my new school, however, I was shocked to hear students speaking to teachers as if they were peers.

Though I didn't imitate them, I got used to the attitudes of students. And the food. But other adjustments would take a bit longer.

Keep Talking

For the first few summer months, before school started, Shari and I spent most of our time around family members who already lived in the States. Having moved from a small island to a sprawling continent, it felt good to be near them. Though most had lived in the States for over a decade, the familiarity felt like home. And because they'd known me my whole life—and because they were *Jamaican*—my cousins, aunts, and uncles had no trouble understanding my thick Jamaican accent.

The first day at Pines Middle School, though, was the first time I ever heard my own accent.

No one teased me. Quite the opposite, in fact. My classmates loved the way I spoke. They were captivated by my speech.

At lunchtime, Shari and I sat with a group of girls who were really nice.

"Keep talking! Keep talking!" they pleaded.

Normally I don't shy away from being the center of attention, but their fascination with me—as if I'd landed in Miami after falling from Jupiter—wasn't the kind of attention I wanted. It felt weird.

It wasn't just the accent, either. Some of the words we used in Jamaica were different too.

Before school one day, I witnessed a fight between two boys in the hallway outside the school gym. It was rough! When a teacher broke it up, sending spectators on to our next classes, I passed a few girls in the hallway who were eager to know what had happened. Feeling like I belonged, I told them what I'd witnessed.

"He tumped him!" I explained.

They looked confused.

"He tumped him!" I repeated, articulating each syllable.

Blank stares.

"What?" they asked in unison.

"You know, *tump*?"

When they continued to stare at me, I pantomimed a punching motion.

"Oh . . ." One girl smiled. "*Punch*! You mean *punch*?" She imitated my air punching.

That's when I learned that *tump*, a Jamaican synonym for "punch," wasn't a word my classmates had ever heard.

I felt so embarrassed.

And I didn't want to stick out again.

So I started watching American movies, studying the dialect of American actors and actresses. I made mental notes that you could "punch" someone, "hit" them, or "deck" them. I also listened to how each word was pronounced.

My *what a gwan* became *what's up*.

My *irie* morphed into *cool*.

And *bredbren* became *bro*.

I became a student of American dialect and, if I don't mind saying, I nailed it.

By the end of middle school, people meeting me for the first time would usually ask, "Are you from New York?"

Hey, what can I say? I watched movies set in the Big Apple!

When I came to America, I wanted nothing more than to blend in. The trouble is that when we try to blend in, we risk losing important parts of ourselves. We can even begin to compromise who we are and what we believe. Thankfully, changing the way I pronounced a few words didn't change the essence of who I was. But I was in need of some kind of anchor that would ground me in the ways that mattered most.

Choices

Figuring out who we are and who we want to be in middle school and high school can be tricky. We want others to notice us, but no one wants to stick out like a sore thumb. Sure, we want to be seen and known, but being *too* different feels like a risk that many of us don't want to take. A lot of young people would rather go along with the crowd than stand up and be who they really are.

I was navigating all the same challenging decisions my friends were facing:

Would I drink alcohol at parties?

Would I smoke cigarettes?

Would I have sex?

Would I smoke pot? (Sometimes people connect "marijuana"

and "Jamaica," but I hadn't even been aware of it until I got to America!)

Because I was always in athletic training, some of those decisions sorted themselves out. Running was too important to me; I didn't want to do anything that could impact my performance. I wasn't willing to suffer the consequences of bad choices by missing meets if I got suspended—by the school or my parents! But more than anything, I respected my body and didn't want to do anything to harm it.

But the decision that would inform all the others is one I made at my aunt Maureen's Caribbean Baptist Church, now ChristWay Baptist, in the fall of 1998.

I always admired my aunt. She and her kids, my cousins Shelley and Kevin, had come to the United States when I was a baby. Aunt Maureen had a peace about her that I deeply respected. After we moved to the U.S., she began taking Shari and me to church several times a week. We went to worship and choir practice and occasional youth events.

But there was a very particular Sunday that would change the trajectory of my life.

I was thirteen, nestled between Shari and Kevin. At the end of the sermon, I clearly remember the pastor asking the most important question I'd ever answer:

"If you died today, would you go to heaven?"

I wasn't sure I would. It's not that I'd done anything so horribly wrong, but I was learning that I could never "earn" my way into heaven. I could never be good *enough*. In order to spend eternity with God, the pastor explained, I needed to receive what Jesus had done for me on the cross and give my life to him.

At the pastor's invitation, with bowed head, I raised my hand to say that I wanted to invite Christ into my heart. Jesus was the anchor I'd been yearning for.

When the pastor invited up those who'd raised our hands, I went forward. The pastor led us in a prayer, and from that moment forward I had complete confidence that my life belonged to Jesus. After some classes with the pastor, I was baptized a month later. To this day I still thank God for claiming me as his own, and I also thank him for the faithful witness of Aunt Maureen, who showed me what it was to live a Christian lifestyle.

She specifically showed me that being a Christian wasn't about "fitting in." That's not who I wanted to be anymore. I wanted to be a young woman who lived a life of faithfulness to Jesus.

Oh, Fork!

By ninth grade, I'd established a reputation on the track. As a result, the seniors on the St. Thomas Aquinas track team (the high school I attended) took me under their wings. I spent more time with them than I did with most ninth graders. I liked it: it was like having a fleet of protective older siblings.

Although I knew they really cared about me, many of my teammates were no angels. A number of them cursed . . . a lot. Cursing wasn't something I'd ever heard in my home, and I wasn't at all comfortable using the kind of language I was hearing. I didn't make a big deal out of it when they cursed, but I also didn't join them.

When we spent time together—in the cafeteria, during practice, or at meets—some of those older kids started to notice that I didn't curse. When someone stepped on my feet with their cleats, I'd squeal, "Shoot, that hurt!" Or if I was extremely outraged, I might say, "Dang!"

At first, they teased me about it. It sort of felt like they thought I was cute—like a puppy. (That isn't what teenage me was hoping for.) But I could tell that some of my friends were trying not to curse so much around me. And I thought that was cool.

We were on the bus riding to a meet one day when the guys in the back started cutting up, the way guys do. One who had a wicked tongue began to say, "What the . . . ?!"

Then I saw him glance over at me and finish his diatribe with, "What the FORK?!"

I could see on his friends' faces that they thought he was nuts.

When his odd outburst left them scratching their heads, he explained, "Gotta keep it clean for my girl, San."

The other guys nodded and accepted his explanation.

After that, I started to hear more of the older kids using clean euphemisms for the ugly words they used to spew out all the time.

Once, when someone told a story that seemed unbelievable, a senior girl queried, "Really? No SHIRT?"

Eventually, every foul word had a clean equivalent. By the

end of freshman year, it had actually become cooler not to curse than to curse.

That experience taught me that I didn't have to go along with what everyone else was doing when I didn't feel it was right. I discovered that when I hung firm, those around me came around and made better choices. Whenever I'd hear one of the silly euphemisms my teammates had started using, I felt very proud to have influenced them for good.

In the face of adversity, though, it doesn't always work out that way.

Bony Legs

Anyone who's seen me race professionally—most likely in the Athens or Beijing or London Olympics—knows that, like the other track and field athletes, I've trained hard to build muscle in my legs, glutes, core, and arms to maximize what I can do on the track. Most would be really surprised to see what I looked like before puberty and before I started taking my training seriously.

In middle school and high school, I was tall and scrawny, with bony elbows and knees. In fact, several kids made fun of the way I looked.

If you've ever had someone tease you for something you couldn't control—the way you looked, or where you lived, or who you lived with, or how much money your family had— you know how much those words can sting. They can really feel brutal.

After school one day, when I was a freshman, a kid from

school who was walking home with his boys looked over at me and snickered. I was stretching, wearing a T-shirt and shorts, waiting for practice to begin.

"Nice bony legs," he jeered, glancing at his friends for their approval.

It was a taunt I'd heard before. Sometimes I let those rude words go, but not this time. I wasn't going to let someone disrespect me.

I retorted, "I know these bony legs are faster than yours!"

Because he knew my reputation as an athlete, he just huffed, "Whatever," and walked away.

He probably didn't want me challenging him to a race and beating him in front of his friends!

Sometimes people will come around and change their ways, like my track team family did. Other times, haters will keep hating. I know that can be really hard. But who other people *think* you are doesn't mean nearly as much as who you *decide* you are.

Even if I hadn't been gifted at running, my faith convinced me that I was precious to God, and my parents let me know that I mattered and I was worth respecting. So instead of believing that I had bony legs, I decided to be fierce. I decided to embrace my faith. And those identities defined me far more than any of my physical qualities ever did.

Investing in You

Throughout high school I honored the promises I'd made to myself about smoking, drinking, drugs, and sex. By keeping the commitments I'd made, I felt I was being true to myself and to God.

Sometimes I hear people call these kinds of choices "sacrifices." I suppose you could look at them that way, but that's not how I see it. I consider making choices that help you reach your goals as "investments," not "sacrifices."

Every time I didn't smoke cigarettes or do drugs, I was investing in the health of my body, because I could see the finish line I was after.

Every time I didn't drink, I was investing in staying healthy and strong to win races.

When I chose to remain a virgin, I was investing in my fidelity to God and to my future spouse.

Every choice was made with the finish line in sight.

As you think about who you want to be today, and how you want to live, first picture the finish line.

For me, that was easy, since my goal as a teen was an actual finish line! But my goal was also my wedding day. My goal was also the day I'd meet God face to face. I wanted to live a life that was pleasing to him every step of the way.

Running the Good Race

What's your finish line?

If your goal is to graduate from college, then you need to be able to see that sunny May graduation day—three years from now or seven years from now—when you throw your black cap in the air and receive your diploma. Seeing the finish line will influence the choices you make today. Will you do the extra credit assignment for history class? Will you play video games after school or will you use that time to study for your exam instead? Will you spend your time and money at the mall, or will you save your money and invest your time in your schoolwork instead?

The future finish line informs who you'll be and how you'll run today.

Perhaps one day you want to marry a wonderful guy with whom you can raise a family. When you look toward the finish line, you probably see a man who's a great husband to you and a great father to your kids. If that's your end game, then you might not want to date the guy who had a lot of drama with his last girlfriend. You probably want to decline a date with the guy who sleeps around. With the finish line in sight, you may choose to stay single awhile longer or to date the kind of guy who you can envision being that great husband and great dad.

The future finish line informs who you'll be and how you'll run today.

Maybe you see yourself starting your own business and succeeding financially so that you can make a difference in your community. If you can see that finish line, then the way you engage your schoolwork *now* matters. The way you spend your allowance *now* matters. The way you volunteer *now* matters. The way you educate yourself on what helps struggling communities *now* matters.

The future finish line informs who you'll be and how you'll run today.

I'm not saying that doing the right thing is always easy. It's not.

But I do believe that in the midst of the pressures you face—to cheat in school, or to experiment with drugs, or to lie to your parents—you have what it takes to walk your own path.

And sometimes, others will even join you on that path.

When you have the courage to be yourself, you impact others for good.

RIGHT ON TRACK CHALLENGE

You'll enjoy the most satisfaction and success in life when you choose to be who you truly are.

- What are some core values or commitments you hold close to your heart?
- Are there people who pressure you to be someone you're not?
- How do you respond?
- What's one time you've chosen to be yourself in the face of pressure?

Take time this week to identify what you value and who you want to be. Write it down, and review it each year on your birthday!

CHAPTER 5

VOICES IN THE CROWD

Several of the track athletes at St. Thomas Aquinas High School had already made names for themselves in South Florida before I came along. They were expected to do great things over the course of their high school years, winning races and meets and medals and titles.

Then I came out of nowhere.

Although I'd been a decorated runner in Jamaica, I was virtually unknown in Florida when we moved to the United States. But by the end of my freshman year, people started to notice. I qualified for the state meet in five events—the 100 and 200 meter races, long jump, high jump, and 4x400 relay—and I won the 100 and 200 races in record-setting times. The *Florida Sun-Sentinel* even named me its female track athlete of the year, one of the youngest to ever receive the distinction.

My first year in high school, there were two other very strong female runners on our team. One, whom I'll call Towanda, was a freshman like me, and the other, whom I'll call Tamika, was an upperclassman. We were great friends, on and off the track. Tamika had won the state championship title the previous year, when I was in middle school.

At the state championships that year, I felt conflicted before the race. I wanted to win, but I also knew how much that would sting for my friend, who'd won the gold as state champion twelve months earlier for her second consecutive title. As we both raced down the track, I gave one hundred percent, like I always do. And as I crossed the finish line, a full stride ahead of Tamika, I glanced over at my friend to see the expression on her face.

Would she be disappointed? Angry? Gracious?

As we both slowed down, Tamika gave me a hug, which felt like a relief. I'd hoped we could continue to be competitors on the track and friends off the track, and her kind embrace signaled that we could.

But as time wore on, the goodwill of my teammates toward me seemed to wane.

Specifically, my teammates seemed to begin gathering around Tamika in a way that excluded me.

No one ever told me to my face of their complicated feelings about being displaced by my arrival, or what it felt like to now be running in my shadow. But the coolness from my teammates seemed to grow as they kept me at a comfortable distance.

At first, I'd get to practice and notice that they'd started warming up without me.

Or I'd notice them lower their voices when I passed by.

After practice, I'd hear them talking about the movie they'd all seen together the previous weekend, and realize they'd chosen not to invite me.

If Shari hadn't been my witness, I might have believed I was just reading too much into the situation, or being too sensitive. But as the distance between me and a few of the girls who'd been my closest friends grew, I began to feel more and more isolated.

Negative People

I think it's natural to want to be seen and known, loved and accepted, for who we are. But all of us will, at some point, face the challenge of negative people in our lives. (I am not saying that my high school track teammates were overtly negative—they never bullied me or directed mean comments my way—but that feeling of being excluded definitely had a negative impact.)

Maybe you've faced resistance from people who envied your success. One teenager I know was excellent at video games. He'd study them until he'd taught himself how to win. But when he always beat his friends at those games, he realized that their reactions made it increasingly less fun to play. Or perhaps you've gotten harassed by people because you *weren't* successful at something. Maybe you struggled in school or had a physical feature that people picked on. You might have heard negative words that really hurt.

What those individuals do and say cannot define you. Only you can decide who you are and who you'll become.

If you look around, you'll probably notice that the people who are able to accept themselves are also happy to encourage and build others up because they're secure in who they are. They don't need to tear someone else down to make themselves feel better. I haven't always been successful at that, but over the years I've tried to support others rather than tear them down.

Heartbreak

The summer after my junior year, I attended the Junior Olympics in Nebraska with the girl who'd been my fiercest rival: my friend Towanda. Though I'd been feeling distant from a number of girls on the team, we really bonded at that meet. I hadn't told anyone on the team about my new crush, but Towanda and I were so tight that summer that I confided in her I had a crush on "Will," the most popular guy on the football team. He was outgoing, handsome, and funny. Even though I knew all the girls liked him, I dared to hope that he'd choose me and we'd start dating in the fall.

On the first day of senior year, I was eager to spot Will in the halls. My hair was long and full because I'd had it straightened for the first time. I was excited for Will to see me because I felt beautiful. On my way to my new locker, though, I saw Towanda, the friend I'd trusted, holding Will's hand. They were walking with some of the guys from the football team and some of the girls from the track team, and they were both beaming. Wide-eyed, I blinked a few times to make sure I wasn't dreaming. My breathing slowed.

When did this happen?
Why hadn't she told me?
Completely blindsided, I was heartbroken.

I wondered if the sinking feeling of rejection I felt was how Towanda had felt every time I won a race.

If she'd wanted me to feel her pain, it worked.

I'm not saying that Towanda had a calculated plan to wound me. I can't say what she was thinking, because I wasn't inside her head. But at the time it felt like a betrayal. It would have hurt a lot even if I hadn't trusted her with my secret, but because I'd exposed such a tender place in my heart, it stung all the more.

Surprise Attack

One of Will's football friends had been flirting with me for weeks, but I wasn't interested in him. My heart was still raw after seeing Towanda with Will, and I wasn't interested in having a new boyfriend.

A few months into our senior year, I was walking from homeroom to first period with Shari and our friend Raecena, when Will's friend passed us and made a sly comment. I actually didn't even hear what he said, but Shari caught whatever snide remark he'd made.

I didn't respond, but Shari sassed back, "Get out of here."

The hallway was packed with students. Towanda wasn't around, but I was aware that Will was with the rest of his crew nearby.

His friend spat back, "You ugly!"

Because he'd been coming on to me for weeks, it kind of felt like he was trying to prove his loyalty to Will.

My classmate's comment raised Shari's hackles, and she and Raecena turned around and retorted, "No, *you* ugly!"

As the argument escalated, Will's friend got more and more upset. Shari and Raecena continued to defend me by pelting the boy with insults. And he shot them right back. As other students paused to watch, I could tell he was getting angrier and angrier.

Then, without warning, he punched me in the face.

My vision blurred. My cheek throbbed.

I had never been punched in the face before, or since!

Shari and Raecena started to push him when a teacher, who'd been close enough to see what was going on, rushed over to break it up.

We all went to the principal's office and I was given a bag of ice. When I called my dad to tell him what had happened, he was outraged. He didn't even finish listening to the story before he was parked on campus.

By the time he arrived, Will's friend was long gone and expelled from school.

I wish that assault meant the end of being on the outs with the people who'd once been such close friends, but it wasn't.

In late winter, Shari, Raecena, and I were at a school social. Our crew of friends wasn't as large as it had been a year earlier, but we were determined to have fun. The new Ludacris song was on, and students were dancing on the gym floor.

Although the boy who'd punched me had been expelled, Will was hanging with a bunch of the other football guys.

One of the players pointed in my direction, shouting out the song lyrics in sync with Ludacris, "You's a hoe, HOE! You's a hoe, HOE!"

What?

Not only had I only dated one guy (and only for about two months), I continued to honor the celibacy promise I'd made at church when I was thirteen. That was a valued part of my identity throughout high school. And their crude remark felt like an emotional assault.

I was humiliated. Although *I* knew the words weren't true, who knows what the other students who were watching thought. I was mortified that something so sacred to me could be abused in such a way. Upon leaving the party, I decided to stick with only attending church gatherings and track meets for the remainder of the year.

Strategy to Combat Negativity

Whenever I felt rejected, betrayed, and harassed, my strategy was to hunker down and focus on what mattered most. I did my schoolwork. I went to church. I trained. I raced. That was my strategy. Thankfully, I had the support of a great family and a few solid friends.

In the race you're running, weathering the impact of negative people requires you to be strategic. You may be in a situation where you need to respond to the negative voices and access outside help. That's what I did after I got hit in the face! But you also may choose to simply ignore the negativity. I did that too. Often if you respond to the negative voices, you waste your energy and end up more exhausted than if you'd just continued running the race in front of you.

The author of Hebrews compares living the Christian life to running a race. Whether or not the writer ever ran around an oval track, he seemed to have a good grasp on how living faithfully is like running a good race. He exhorts, "Let us run with perseverance the race marked out for us, fixing our eyes on Jesus, the pioneer and perfecter of faith" (Hebrews 12:1–2). The passage then continues to describe Jesus's fortitude in enduring the suffering of the cross to finish well. The critical message to hang on to is just five words: "fixing our eyes on Jesus."

The temptation, for all of us who are hearing negative voices, is to tip our ears and eyes toward those voices and faces. But no good comes from giving them our energy and attention. The real win, in any circumstance, is to fix our eyes on Jesus.

That kind of focus is a critical strategy in racing well. Whenever I was tempted to focus on the runners beside me, behind me, or in front of me, that's when I would falter. Stumble. Burn out. But when I kept my mind fixed on running the race with faithfulness, always holding the finish line in my heart, that's when I ran my best races.

When other students acted negatively toward me, I had to choose how I'd handle it. I'm not saying it was easy, but by focusing on what I knew I needed to do—school, church, track—I could run my race with perseverance and not get bogged down by others' words and attitudes.

Senior year wasn't the only time I'd faced haters. I'd go on to confront plenty of other negativity through the years. I faced jeering crowds and received ugly emails. I dealt with a challenging coach. I navigated a relationship with an agent I wasn't convinced had my best interests at heart. Along the way there were lots of negative voices in the crowd.

When our eyes are fixed on what matters most, when we're anchored in Jesus, we can rise above negative people.

Who are the negative people in your life?

Maybe you face difficult people at school, like I did. Maybe you have a sibling who won't give you a break. Maybe there are adults in your home, or family, who aren't able to encourage you and support you.

You do not need to be a victim of the negativity of others. I believe you have all the resources you need to choose the good way, and to rise above the negativity.

Whatever you're facing today, imagine me in the stands cheering for you.

RIGHT ON TRACK CHALLENGE

When you're purposing to be the best you that you can be, you may face negativity from those around you.

- Who are the people who recognize and cherish who you are?
- Who are the negative voices in your life right now?
- What does your internal voice say about who you are?

- What does God say about your identity and value and purpose?

You have what it takes to rise above negativity. What strategies will you use this week?

_____

CHAPTER 6

WINS AND LOSSES

When I was invited to join the junior national track team—a team of the best runners under the age of nineteen from across the United States—I was ecstatic. I loved competing locally and regionally, but to represent my country meant the world to me.

The process of registering for the team required a copy of my passport. That's when my mom and I realized that I didn't have one! We were legal immigrants, with a green card to live and work in the United States, but we weren't naturalized citizens.

It was the first time I felt like I had to choose between my Jamaican roots and the country that had become home to me. All my friends were American, and I wanted to make the team with them. Though it had only been four years since I'd competed in Jamaica, I didn't know any of the young Jamaican athletes.

America had become home.

I begged my parents to let me join Team USA. It wasn't an easy decision at all; my family had many discussions about it. We're proud Jamaicans, but, in the end, my parents thought the best decision for my future was to compete as an American.

Because Shari and I would become U.S. citizens when my mom was naturalized, she started working toward her citizenship right away. Most natural-born Americans don't realize the rigor of the process. There's a lot of learning, vetting, and preparing that goes into it. Instead of Mom quizzing me on my American history, I was quizzing her! I knew she was working toward gaining U.S. citizenship just for me, and I wanted to help her as much as I could. I was thrilled when she'd jumped through all the hoops and we became United States citizens.

In the years after we became citizens, and I began competing for the U.S., people often expected me to offer a deep, philosophical reason for my decision. Honestly, I was sixteen; I'd been in the U.S. for four years and all my friends were American. My family also believed it was best for my future. As we discussed it around our dinner table, it just made *sense*.

Some of the world's greatest athletes have opted to compete for countries they were not born into. Donovon Bailey and Linford Christie were both Jamaican-born sprinters who went on to win Olympic gold at 100 meters for their adopted countries. Bailey represented Canada while Christie represented Great Britain.

I believed that we'd made the right decision. But because I had always internalized being very loved as a young athlete in Jamaica, I couldn't foresee the controversy our choice would cause.

Back to Jamaica

The year I joined the team, the World Junior Championships—presented by the International Association of Athletics Federations—were hosted in Kingston, Jamaica.

They'd never been hosted in Jamaica before, and they never have since!

The opportunity felt like a gift. My international debut would unfold on a stage where I had so many cherished memories. I looked forward to racing in the country that had shaped me as a runner and competitor. I was scheduled to compete in the 200, 400, 4x100, and 4x400—the only female athlete entered in four events on Team USA.

I had been given this amazing opportunity because I had won the 200 and 400 meters at the U.S. Junior Nationals, which was no easy feat. Set to race two of the best up-and-coming sprinters in the country, I ended up beating Monique Henderson and breaking her national high school record by running 50.69, which still stands today. I also defeated Allyson Felix in a tight finish in the 200 meters. Still riding the high of my best meet ever, I was eager to compete in Kingston.

But I did understand that some Jamaicans would have mixed feelings about me. Before leaving home, the junior squad of Team USA voted me team captain and elected me to serve as flag bearer in the opening ceremonies. I was flattered, but, knowing my presence in Jamaica as an American athlete might cause strong emotions for and against me, I told them I didn't want to offend the Jamaican fans. I declined the honor.

A day before the competition began, about one hundred and twenty American athletes descended on Kingston, traveling in our blue warm-up suits with the signature red stripe on the side. As I stepped out of the jet bridge into the Kingston airport, I began to feel nervous about how I might be received.

I first felt the pressure of my decision the afternoon we arrived, during a press conference designed to preview the games. The media event featured, among others, a young Jamaican hopeful named Usain Bolt. I could hear the negative edge in the voices of interviewers pummeling me with questions about my choice to represent the United States rather than Jamaica. As the day wore on, I could feel my nerves fraying. One newspaper quoted me as saying, "I hope everybody will still love me."

Yet my hoping did not make it so.

Many Jamaicans felt as though I'd abandoned my homeland. Instead of the warmth and affection I'd dreamed of, my arrival on Jamaican soil was met with hostility.

I thought that not carrying the flag would have been the biggest disappointment of the games.

I was wrong.

Crushing Reception

Though viewers watching televised races from home only see the main track, there's also a warm-up track beside the main one, where racers prepare for competition. As I stretched beside National Stadium, I prayed and asked God to quiet my heart and mind. I'd felt uneasy throughout the day, but I focused on keeping my head in the game as I warmed up with my teammates.

When it was time, I slipped off my sweats in the call room and was handed a paper number that I pinned to my uniform. An official lined us up and we were escorted through a tunnel and into the main stadium.

As we jogged out onto the track, ugly booing erupted in the stands. Surely, I reasoned, that was for someone else, for something happening elsewhere in the stadium. Still, I continued to feel uncomfortable.

I was particularly anxious as the announcer began announcing the contestants, lane by lane.

"And in lane five, representing the United States of America . . . Sanya Richards!"

The booing that ensued across the stadium confirmed my worst fears: I was unwelcome.

Shari, who'd come to support me, burst into tears in the stands. I, though, didn't have the leisure for tears. Since I was in the public eye, I took a deep breath and gathered as much courage as I could muster. Raising my arm to wave to the hostile crowd, I vowed that I wouldn't cry.

Jamaicans ridiculed my family. They jeered. They sent me ugly emails. It wasn't the generation of Jamaicans my age who had the problem with me—it was older ones who saw me as a traitor. These were Jamaicans who'd followed the sport for several decades, and who'd seen my potential when I was a girl.

My dad had played soccer for the Jamaica national junior team, and they believed he'd done the wrong thing by allowing me to compete for the U.S. It was a bit ironic, since many of those Jamaican fans lived in the United States like we did! Honestly, Shari and my mom and I second-guessed the decision to become U.S. citizens after we realized we'd be letting people down. But my dad was always adamant. He felt strongly that it had been a good decision because my sister and I could take advantage of the rich opportunities available in the U.S.

Facing negativity among my teammates and classmates had been difficult, but this challenge was at a whole new level.

Giving It My All

As had become par for the course, I was scheduled to compete in a lot of races. I was supposed to run the 200 and the 400, as well as the 4x100 and the 4x400 relays. Between all the preliminary and final heats, it was a very heavy load.

By the afternoon of the second day, I knew I'd made it into the finals of the 400. The opening heat of the 200, though, was scheduled just a few hours before the 400 finals.

Had I been a more seasoned runner, I would have approached that sequence more strategically. But, being young and energetic, I hadn't yet faced my body's limits.

Standing on the track where my journey had begun, my mind flooded with the Jamaican win-or-lose mentality: *If you come in second, you're the first loser.* In the opening heats, though, a runner only had to come in first or second to advance to the next round. Ideally, I should have paced myself and been content with a second-place finish that would have moved me forward the same way a win would have.

But I was intent on winning it all, even the prelims.

In the 200 prelims, I raced against a Canadian runner who ran the best race of her life against me. The two of us were far ahead of the rest of the runners in our heat. But rather than sliding easily into second place behind her, I powered through to beat her in the first round. She was so fast that I had to set my own personal best to do it too!

That obsession, that naivety about running strategy, wouldn't serve me well.

She Nah Go Win!

That afternoon, the finals of the 400 came quicker than I would have chosen.

More than fifteen thousand fans were crammed inside National Stadium. Steel drum beats and the black-green-and-gold flags of Jamaica rose into the muggy night air from the sea of people. Jamaicans love track and field and are very rarely rewarded with international-caliber competition, so this event meant a lot to the people and the country. Every fan wanted to see the Jamaicans win. But unlike my Vaz Prep days, I was not in the right colors.

As I lined up beside my teammate, Monique Henderson, the heckling grew louder.

"She nah go win!"

"She's a sellout!"

"She don't deserve di gold."

Jamaica's fans were merciless in their criticism.

Even though I was treated as the adversary, forced to line up as the villain for the first time, my focus didn't waver. Like every other time I entered a race, I was set on winning.

My mind and heart were ready, but my legs couldn't hold up their end of the bargain.

I ran hard and felt strong. For the first half of the race, Monique and I ran neck and neck. But when I came into the last 100 meters, there was nothing left. My energy was gone, drained from me on this same spot a few hours earlier, with that crazy kick to conquer my 200 heat.

Now, when it mattered, in the 400 final—when a winner was actually determined—I couldn't find another gear to match my American teammate, Monique. I looked over at her midway down the homestretch in disappointment as she passed me.

I suddenly had a keen understanding of how my high school teammates Tamika and Towanda may have felt when I'd beaten them.

I was devastated.

Just past the finish line, I found Monique and hugged her in congratulations, then found a nearby chair and slumped into it. I was exhausted and humiliated. As I stared at the track, I berated my effort. I wanted to win. I wanted to set a personal record. I wanted to prove to the people who sneered and jeered me that I was at least worth the effort, and that I lived up to my billing. That Team USA was lucky to have me.

But I didn't do any of that, and I had to be back at the track the next morning for my 200 semifinal.

To add injury to insult, after the 200 semifinal I sprained my ankle during the preliminary heats of the 4x400 relay. I wasn't even supposed to compete in that race. I was in the stands in my jeans and T-shirt, supporting one of my teammates, when another teammate had to drop out due to injury and I needed to step in. I wasn't prepared at all. I borrowed a uniform and some spikes and ran the race. Our team had a great race, and we won the heat.

Unfortunately, after crossing the finish line first, I stepped into a hole on the side of the track—which was disguised by tall grass—and severely rolled my ankle. I'd later learn that seasoned runners know never to step into the infield. With the possibility of equipment lying around, or hidden holes, it's just too risky.

I went down to Jamaica with sights set on a pair of individual gold medals, but left with none. Flying home with a silver in the 400 and bronze in the 200, I was beaten, mentally and physically.

It was a difficult international debut to say the least.

Redeeming Losses

I learned the hard way that it's possible to be successful in many areas and still face failures. They're bitterly painful in the moment, but I'm convinced that they also offer opportunities for growth.

What I learned from my defeat on the track gave me

insights I couldn't have learned any other way. A coach could have told me that I shouldn't spend everything in the prelims, but that horribly public failure was how I learned it for myself.

I'm not saying it's easy. Losing can be brutal. Losing a competition stings. Bombing your SAT or ACT can feel devastating. Failing to reach whatever goal you've set for yourself—managing your weight, auditioning for a play, applying for an afterschool job—can feel awful. But when you face the disappointment of losing, and decide to learn something from your loss, you develop resilience and become better able to navigate setbacks in the future. Maybe you learn, like I did, when to power up and when to dial back. Maybe you learn what you need to study to get the score you want on a test. I'm convinced that every loss offers the possibility for learning that contributes to future success.

I know I learned from my loss in Kingston. About ten years later, in Istanbul, I had two 400 meter races on the same day. I was faced with a situation similar to the one I faced in Jamaica. I could have powered through to win in the prelims, but I knew to do that was to risk a loss in the finals. Because I'd learned from that early loss, I chose to dial it back in the prelims and run conservatively. Then, in the finals, I had all I needed to win. That subsequent victory wouldn't have been possible if I'd stubbornly continued to repeat my mistakes. But because I wanted to improve, I was able to learn from my loss, recalibrate my strategy, and continue on to success.

In the weeks after my loss in Kingston, though, I was gripped with disappointment.

Recovery

A few weeks after I'd returned from Jamaica, still disappointed, my mom let me know that I'd been invited to a press event for a local newspaper. So I put on my favorite dress, a lime green sundress, and hopped into the car with her. For some reason the photo was scheduled to be taken at a local hotel.

When we entered the hotel, I saw one of my uncles! Weird coincidence, right? It felt like a surprise party situation, but my birthday wasn't for seven more months.

After my mother led me down the hall, she threw open the doors to the ballroom and I saw a huge banner that read "Sanya Richards Day."

What?!

A room full of people were beaming and applauding me. When the shock wore off, and I began to mingle with family and friends and coaches, I learned that the St. Thomas Athletics Director, George Smith, and my high school coach, John Guarino, had organized the surprise event to announce me as the 2002 Gatorade National High School Girls Athlete of the Year.

So, technically, a photographer eventually did take my picture for the paper.

In conjunction with the City of Fort Lauderdale and our congressman, July 25, 2002 was officially named Sanya Richards Day. I even received a congratulatory letter from Florida governor Jeb Bush.

Other Floridians had been named athlete of the year, but I was the state's first track and field student-athlete recipient. Looking back today, the timing of the honor felt fortuitous. It fueled my fire again and motivated me to live up to the expectations of those who recognized both my past accomplishments and my future potential. In the weeks to come, I'd picture that glorious ballroom during the most grueling parts of my workout!

I'd still been feeling disappointed by what had happened in Jamaica that summer. But the Sanya Richards Day event that had been in the works before I ever set foot in Kingston's National Stadium was a great reminder that I was not, and never would be, defined by my losses. No one's life will ever be all gold medals. The most impressive champions—Usain Bolt, Simone Biles, Michael Phelps, Gabby Douglas—have all faced personal defeats. Even in the wake of defeat, though, you can carry yourself like a champion.

That's what I tried to do after losing in Kingston: I held my head high and continued to walk, and run, with dignity.

RIGHT ON TRACK CHALLENGE

Everyone faces losses. Your challenge is to learn from them.

- What have been your biggest losses?
- What happened to make you feel like a "loser"?
- How did you respond?

- What can you learn from your loss that will help you in the future?

Not every endeavor yields a win. But you can transform losses by learning from them.

CHAPTER 7

RUN YOUR BEST RACE

An athlete is considered "amateur" as long as she hasn't received money for competing. So although I'd raced in the 2004 Olympics while I was enrolled as a student at University of Texas, I was still considered an amateur athlete. But I knew that the minute I received my first dollar for running, I'd be ineligible to race for the university.

The decision to turn professional wasn't one that my family and I took lightly. I'd attended college, as many students do, both to get a better idea of the job I'd enjoy and to prepare myself for the work I'd pursue. And, as it is with a few other careers—child actors, other young athletes, precocious entrepreneurs—I was in a position to begin the job I loved *before* I finished my education, rather than after.

We all know the window during which a professional athlete can compete is typically short. Though the average retirement age in the United States is sixty-two, the overwhelming majority of hockey players who play in the NHL retire in their twenties. The average age of retirement for football players in the NFL is thirty. The average age of retirement for basketball players in the NBA is thirty-six.

When I was in my early teens, I felt like I had my whole

life to compete and to win. But my parents saw that window very differently. They realized we had to be smart about the decisions we were making about my career as a track athlete.

Knowing when athletes retire begs the question of when we're at our peak. A study from the Institute of Biomedical Research and Sports Epidemiology in France revealed that, although gender and athletic event do make a difference, the average age at which track and field athletes peak is twenty-six! Though I was still climbing toward my peak at nineteen, the statistics were sobering.

So, guided by prayer and conversation with my family and coaches, I decided to forgo my college eligibility as an athlete in order to make room to do the thing I loved and had been born to do: train and compete on the international stage.

In fact, I did continue attending school for an additional year, and my sponsor, Nike, picked up my tuition. It was a lot of work, and my races did require that I miss a number of classes, but I knew how to study and carved out time to do it on airplanes and in hotel rooms.

In 2005, I began my first full year competing as a professional athlete.

Though I'd attended the World Championships before, I was very excited to be attending them for the first time as a pro athlete. By turning pro, I finally had the opportunity to win a cash prize. In the fall of 2005, I was eager to run my best race for Team USA in Helsinki, Finland.

My fiercest competitor was Tonique Williams from the Bahamas. She was already an Olympic champion, having won gold in the 400 in Athens in 2004. Heading into Helsinki, she and I had both been named among the favorites. And during the other meets in 2004, Tonique had only been beat by one person.

Me.

I'd overtaken her in the 400 at Lausanne, and I'd eked past her at Sheffield as well. But the reality was that I was still only nineteen years old in my first year as a professional athlete. Although my times were competitive with Tonique's, it would still be a long shot to beat her on the world stage.

Helsinki

Because Olympic fans watching televised coverage of the most prestigious games see Team USA marching together in our red, white, and blue in the opening ceremonies, or cheering on teammates who've made it to the podium, many assume that we all spend time training together and developing bonds throughout the year. And although we do have the opportunity to forge friendships at competitions, many of us are meeting each other for the first time in those games—even members of relay teams who need to work together seamlessly.

Over one hundred athletes on Team USA had flown out of New York's LaGuardia Airport on a chartered plane to Finland. We were a sight to behold as we poured out of the plane onto a Helsinki runway in our red-and-navy warm-up suits.

But traveling with the U.S. team meant that I wasn't traveling with those closest to me. I didn't sit next to Shari on the plane. I didn't fly with my parents. And even Coach Hart didn't travel beside me. Instead, my family and coach traveled separately while I flew with national team members, which included athletes, managers, and coaches for Team USA. It was a fun experience, but I missed my personal coach and family.

We landed in Europe a day before my first prelim. I ran well in the early rounds of the 400, and I knew I'd still have something left to give in the finals.

After coming in first in my semifinal round, I returned to the warm-up track that's situated beside the competition track. I was doing my cooldown routine, along with other teammates, under the watchful eye of my personal coach. As I was jogging around the familiar oval, I was visualizing the race I'd run the next day.

Though every race is unique, I knew exactly whose body would be closest to mine the following day.

Tonique's.

Having competed against her many times, including several that year, I could imagine how she'd run her race. I knew her posture, I understood her pacing, and I could even anticipate when she'd turn on her power. While it helped to know how she might race, my most important job was to implement the strategy Coach Hart and I had designed.

I could see our plan in my mind. I'd burst off the blocks and hit my four Ps—push, pace, position, and poise.

Crouched over the track, feet staggered, I'd explode off the blocks in an effort to reach maximum speed in just several steps. Pushing forward, I'd be launched into my next steps by the track itself.

After that first one hundred-yard push, I'd throttle back to take in the oxygen my body needs and stretch into the best tempo for my stride. I'd find the rhythm that is uniquely mine.

By the time I rounded the final turn, I would be thinking about the position I wanted to be in for the final one hundred meters of the race. This third phase of positioning was the first time I even needed to consider where my competitors were situated. I would become aware of everything going on around me.

The final hundred meters require poise. My muscles had been trained to do their job, and that last stretch required as much from my head as it did from my legs. It's that point at which runners' bodies are most likely to lose their form and begin to flail. In the final one-hundred, my mind's job was to remind my body to do what it had been trained to do. That poise requires concentration. And for me, prayer.

Coach Hart and I had agreed that I wouldn't hit full throttle until the last 110 meters of the race. That was the pattern that had been effective in Lausanne and Sheffield, both times that I'd beaten Tonique that year.

A Fresh Strategy

As my cooldown jog slowed to a walk, an athlete I considered a legend in our sport began walking beside me. I'll call him James. James was a decorated athlete, more than a decade my senior, and I really admired all that he'd accomplished. Yeah, maybe I was even a little starstruck. I was honored that he was taking the time to help me consider the race I'd run the next day.

"If you want to win," he said, "you've got to come off the final turn first, and then just hold it."

As he was speaking, I was picturing some of his victories I'd seen in person and on television. I knew exactly the kind of lengthy final push he was describing. I'd seen him run that race successfully many times.

Coach Hart was just fifty meters away, probably pleased to see that I was being shepherded by the best of the best. But I also knew that this older runner, who had much more experience than me, wasn't describing the race Coach Hart and I had agreed I'd run.

But I was young, I was relatively inexperienced, and I was hungry for this win.

And I knew, from all my other races against Tonique in 2005, that this race could go either way. I was desperate to show the world that I was the best. That desperation meant I wasn't willing to trust that the race Coach and I had planned out was the best race for me.

What I wanted was *magic*. I wanted to believe that there was something outside of me, something greater, something bigger, that would be the key to a win. I now know that impulse—to find a magic bullet outside of ourselves—is what causes people to make poor choices. They stop believing that hard work and smart strategy is enough. They succumb to the temptation to believe that something outside of themselves will be the ticket to the win they've been training for.

Looking for the Win

I know I'm not alone.

The student who slips a cheat sheet up his sleeve during a French quiz has bought into the lie that he can't, or won't, succeed without extra help.

The candidate who stuffs the ballot box to ensure a victory—for homecoming queen, or club president, or team captain—has swallowed the lie that "the win" is worth sacrificing her integrity.

The young person who's caught stealing cash from a teacher's desk has somehow convinced himself that whatever he gains is justified.

And though I wasn't breaking any rules by changing up my race strategy, I'd agreed to the lie that the win could only be secured by a trick or spell or potion or magic outside of myself.

That's what we do sometimes, right? We complicate things by trying to find something outside of ourselves to be our comfort, our hope, our victory, our salvation. If that temptation sounds familiar, it's because it's what we do when we fail to completely trust God with our lives. But when we ultimately decide to turn our lives over to God, and not just attempt to manipulate him into getting what we want, we'll finally experience the peace that comes from trusting him.

I was still considering the strategy James had suggested as I walked off the track that day.

As I headed toward the locker room, Coach asked, "You guys have a good chat?"

"Yes," was all I said.

That night as I lay awake in bed visualizing my race for the next day, I was picturing my body running the race that had been so successful for my teammate.

Race Day

Dark clouds hung in the sky the next morning. Though it was only drizzling when I woke up, a torrential downpour began as I reached the track. Wind whipped sheets of rain against all the runners as we stretched and ran our warm-up laps. As long as there was no lightning, we knew the race was on. My coach, who had been active in the sport for over fifty years, had never seen anything like it. I was already mentally reviewing my strategy, and the distraction of the weather wasn't helping at all.

I was assigned to lane 3, and Tonique was in lane 6. That meant that there were two lanes to my left on the inside of the track, two runners between myself and Tonique, and two lanes to Tonique's right on the outside of the track. Because the start locations are staggered to account for the rounded lanes, the runner in lane 1 is positioned the farthest back and is able to keep all of the other runners in view until she passes them. The runner in the farthest lane, lane 8, is "running blind" until she is passed by runners on the inside lanes. My spot in lane 3 meant that for the first several hundred meters, I would have a sense of where Tonique was.

After we were all announced, we crouched down to position ourselves for the start of the race. The downpour had eased up, but rain was still falling on the track.

Bang!

With the familiar gunshot, we were off and running!

For the first two hundred meters, I was comfortable with Tonique being "ahead" of me in lane 6. I knew that when the lanes evened out for the last one hundred meters, we'd most likely be neck and neck. Any "lead" she had until then wasn't meaningful.

But as I went into the final turn, James's words rang in my ears: *"You've got to come off the final turn first, and then just hold it."*

His words sounded so simple.

Eager to implement them, I turned up the juice and passed Tonique halfway through the turn, with just over one hundred meters to go.

"You've got to come off the final turn first . . ."

I'd done it. I'd come off the turn first!

His words continued to echo: *". . . and then just hold it."*

That was more difficult.

As my spikes dug into the wet track, I felt myself pushing, pushing, pushing.

As I entered the home stretch, a lot of people in the stands thought I was going to beat Tonique. But with each step, I realized I hadn't executed my race.

I *willed* my body to move faster, but I could feel my legs giving way beneath me. My body had stopped responding to my heart and mind. With sixty meters left, I knew that I'd burned up the energy I needed to sustain the pace needed for victory. Though all the runners were still behind me, I caught a glimpse of Tonique passing me on the outside with just forty meters left in the race. I had nothing left, and followed her to the finish line.

Tonique, who'd felt the pressure of the race as deeply as I had, fell to her knees at the finish line.

I realized the moment I crossed the finish line in Tonique's shadow that I'd not run my race. I felt like I'd betrayed my coach. I'd run someone else's race, and had failed.

I was crushed. After congratulating Tonique, I left the track as quickly as I could. As I tried to escape, the first person I saw was Coach Hart. I collapsed into his arms and bawled.

"What are you crying for?" he asked me, incredulously. "You're a world silver medalist!"

Perhaps if I'd done all that I was supposed to do, if I'd run *my* race, those words would have soothed me.

"Put your chin up," he instructed me. "You have no reason to be crying."

A light rain now sprinkling the track, I limped along with his arm around me, taking deep breaths to stop my sobbing.

I *knew* that I'd messed up.

Lesson Learned

When I executed my own race, I was golden. I'd been able to beat Tonique twice because I'd implemented the strategy Coach and I had agreed on.

But when I tried to execute someone else's race, I fell short.

Since I learned that hard lesson, I've noticed the same phenomenon again and again at the track. I've seen runners give too much too early, and not have enough left at the end of the race. Or I've seen them save up so much energy and lose so much ground that there's no way to catch the leader when they finally do turn up the heat at the end. And because I know what it is to be running with someone else's voice in my head—even the voice of an older champion athlete!—I understand the temptation to try something different in hopes it will make a difference.

But I also see the same phenomenon in women and girls *off* the track.

When I notice someone trying to be someone they're not, often to impress others, it usually ends up coming off as a fail. If they're trying to act tougher, or flirtier, or smarter, or happier than they really are, it *shows*. If they're trying to be Beyoncé or Miley or Tyra, they're not being who they were made to be.

But when I encounter a woman or girl being who she really is, she radiates something that is genuine and real.

Though I don't think I could pull off blue hair, I've seen women who *rock* blue hair like they were born with it! I've seen girls and women wearing brightly colored wraps who are, under that flourish of color, clearly being who they were made to be.

That's been true for me on the track, and it's also been

true for me off the track. Whether I'm in my pajamas at home with my family or glitzed up for the red carpet, I have the most confidence when I'm being Sanya. Trying to be like someone else is never a win.

I see it in fashion, but I also see it in *passion*.

If your sister was passionate about skating, you might have tried to glide right behind her in lessons or practices or competitions. It could be that you're also a gifted skater, but it's also possible you'll end up finding the most satisfaction by pursuing something different.

We can all be tempted to try and be someone we're not, especially when we spend a lot of time on social media. Whether it's what Kylie is wearing, or Jennifer is singing, or Staci is performing, or Tamika is driving, we're tempted to be what we're not by imitating what we think is working for others.

In every area of life—faith, fashion, passions, pursuits, beauty, and later your career—we can be tempted to imitate someone else, instead of focusing on running the unique race that only we can run.

I encourage you to ask God how you're being invited to run *your* race. And I've found the best way to do that is double-pronged, and may seem counterintuitive!

First, you have to get quiet. We live in a noisy world, and God invites us to pop out the earbuds, turn down the volume on our distractions, and be still with him. Spend some quiet time alone with God and have a conversation about the ways you're uniquely made. Grab your Bible, pull out a journal, and listen for God's still, small voice. Begin to notice the ways God has created you to thrive, and ask God what makes you uniquely you.

In addition to being still, I also encourage you to get busy! Continue to step out and try new things. Find out which ones energize you and which ones drain you. Which ones make you happy and which ones exhaust you. Join a friend one week at her piano lesson, her soccer practice, or her church's youth group! Record what you notice in your journal, and continue to ask God for guidance.

Because no two people on the planet are identical, you are like no other.

Run the race that only you can run.

RIGHT ON TRACK CHALLENGE

Do you have a sense of what it looks like to run the race that only you can run, to be the person that only you can be?

- What values are most important to you?
- What are some goals that you've set for yourself?
- What are the dreams you hold in your heart?
- What kind of activities make you feel alive and give you joy?

Though you might be tempted to follow in the footsteps of others, you were made to live a life that's unique to you! What will you do today to stay in your lane?

CHAPTER 8

EYES ON THE FINISH LINE

In 2006, which had been the best year of my career to date, my dad was pushing me to chase the American record for the women's 400-meter run. That record was 48.83 seconds. It had been set by Valerie Brisco-Hooks in Los Angeles in 1984, and I was itching to break it. My dad was eager for me to do so too.

Up until that race, my own lifetime best race had been 48.92. I'd run it in August of 2005 at the Weltklasse in Zurich. As the 2006 season was underway, I was running so well during most of my races that I peeked over at the clock before crossing the finish line.

And that was exactly what my dad wanted to discuss the day before the World Cup in Athens, Greece two months later.

Though I often had a huge cheering section of family and friends at stadiums around the globe, only my mom had traveled with me to Athens. The night before the finals, when I was Skyping with my dad, he brought up what was—by the clock—the best race I'd ever won.

But as he and I had watched it together back at home a few months earlier, he'd noticed something.

Reviewing the Race

We'd been sitting together on the couch.

"See!" he pointed. "Right there!"

He was showing me the slightest movement of my eyes as I glanced up at the clock during my race. I don't mean that I turned my head to look at a runner beside me or behind me. I don't mean that I raised my arms to wave at anyone in the stands or stumbled into someone else's lane. I mean that my *eyes* moved. There might have been the slightest shift of my head as my eyes drifted over to look at the clock.

The way I saw it, I'd been running so well, beating everyone else on the track, that the clock became my competition. Why not peek for that extra inspiration to give it everything I had?

But in that slight movement of my eyes, my dad noticed that my body would stiffen. My shoulders tensed up after I looked at the clock.

Ironically, in that moment, I wanted to roll my eyes. But my dad's pretty sharp. And I knew he was probably right.

Race Eve

We'd scheduled a Skype call the evening before my finals in Athens. It was one o'clock in the afternoon in Florida, and eight o'clock in the evening in Greece. Though I'd run my prelims without any trouble, my body was still adjusting to the time zone. And I wanted to be well rested for the next day.

We were chatting about the day and the food and what

was happening with Shari, when my dad returned to that eye-gaze business.

"Darling," my dad begged me, "please. Do it for me. I promise you, you won't be sorry."

"Dad," I retorted, "my mechanics are fine. My form is fine. It's just not that big of a deal."

I heard his sigh around the globe.

"San," he reasoned with me, "if you just keep your eyes forward, I promise you'll gain speed. It's slowing you down."

They were the words I'd been hearing him say all season long.

"You have nothing to lose. Just try it my way. Promise me you won't look at the clock, and you'll be happy."

Race Day

The night before each race, I fall asleep without setting an alarm. I always want to give my body as much rest as possible by allowing it to wake when it wants to. My eyes closed for the night around ten and I didn't wake up until eight in the morning!

Because I wasn't scheduled to race until seven that night, my mom and I had a pretty chill day together. We enjoyed a leisurely breakfast, read for a while, and watched a race on television before I took a bath and got dressed to head to the stadium.

On one hand, I wasn't particularly nervous for the race, since I'd been undefeated that season. I was ranked number one in the world. I expected to wrap up a really good season with a win in Athens.

On the other hand, I was going to be running in lane 7. In the 400, it's usually better to be in lane 4 or 5 to keep the competition in view. In lane 7, I knew I'd be running blind, hoping not to give too much too soon. I'd never been in lane 7 before in a major meet.

What I thought might be a deficit—not being able to see how my performance compared to that of other runners—turned out to be a benefit! I'd learned to run my own race and now I was being given a chance to put my learning into practice!

Coming off the final turn, I couldn't place the other runners with my peripheral vision. Though I couldn't see them, I never turned my head to look. What my mom saw from the stands was that, as I came out of the turn, the closest runner was about ten meters behind me. I focused on my fourth "P," staying poised, and continued to run strong for the last one hundred meters. And though I wouldn't see it until I watched the race later on film, I was even adding to the distance between me and the other runners in the final forty meters.

For four hundred meters, I refused to look at the clock.

I did it for my daddy.

In the last twenty meters, whatever the stadium's announcer was saying in Greek didn't even matter to me. I felt great and was clearly poised for the win. Feeling my strength beneath me, powering forward but with enough gas in the tank for a strong finish, I won!

A Greek runner who'd come in second congratulated me.

She actually grabbed my face, and as we both reached for a quick hug, we almost kissed on the mouth! Although it was awkward, it felt like one of the most authentic congratulations I've ever received from a competitor. Normally competitors aren't happy when you beat them, but she was a hurdler, and had been a last-minute substitution in the 400, so she was less invested than everyone else.

After her hug, I was handed a beautiful bouquet of flowers by a girl dressed in traditional Greek garb.

As I continued to steady my breath, I glanced up at the clock. By then, I wasn't interested in the win; I was interested in the time!

When the times were shown, I realized that the U.S. Women's record of 48.83, that had stood for twenty-two years, had been broken.

I'd run the race in 48.7 seconds.

Keeping my eyes off the clock, and on the race, had shaved a third of a second off my own personal best, and thirteen one-hundredths off the U.S. women's record.

I know that thirteen one-hundredths of a second sounds pretty small. But for me, it was huge. It was a big deal to the sport too. The American records have been set by some of the best athletes in human history . . . and I'd smashed the record! That year I would be named World Athlete of the Year and American Athlete of the Year.

I was ecstatic!

But in the moment, I didn't know if 48.7 would mean much to anyone besides me. There was no reason that the

European crowd would have been familiar with the American record.

But my mom knew what 48.7 meant.

I searched the stadium, desperate to make eye contact with her. I finally found her waving her arms in celebration.

As soon as we got back to the hotel, we called my dad.

"Dad, I did it! I did it! I broke the record. Forty-eight point seven seconds! It felt awesome!"

"Did you look at the clock?" he queried playfully.

"No," I admitted. "I didn't."

He'd been right.

Eyes on the Prize

Before September 16, 2006, I had run countless thousands, even millions, of steps. I'd put in the miles and the crunches and the lifting and the strategizing to become a champion. But what finally got me across the finish line in lightning speed was taking my eyes off my competition—whether it was Tonique Williams or a huge glowing digital clock—and keeping my eyes and heart and mind on the goal.

In my case, it wasn't the literal "prize" I was eyeing. I had other gold medals. It was staying focused on the race I was running. It was the finish line.

When we set goals for ourselves, it's easy to get distracted from what we've set our minds to do.

Maybe you're eyeballing the musician who's nipping at your heels to win first chair in the orchestra. Maybe you're looking down at the numbers on a scale. Maybe you're doing excellent work at your part-time job, but you sneak off to count your tips. Or maybe you've set an academic goal for yourself, and halfway through the semester you simply get tired.

I get that. I really do.

You might even lose focus, like I did when I looked at the clock, with good reasons in mind. But just like my race in Athens, you'll achieve the most success when you're not distracted and keep your mind focused on the goals you've set for yourself.

I've known girls who've gotten distracted by guys. I don't mean there's anything wrong with dating someone. I mean that they've settled for someone who's not the caliber of person they should be dating. Or they've decided to date someone who doesn't respect the goals and values and priorities that they've chosen for themselves. I've known girls who've dated guys who demanded so much of their time and attention that they weren't able to develop into the women they'd been designed to be.

I've also known girls who've gotten distracted by focusing on their appearance. You know I'm a girlie girl, and I love stylish hair, unique nails, and fashion, so I don't mean that there's anything wrong with putting effort into your appearance. But when girls become consumed by what they look like, they forget their higher calling and more important goals! Those goals might not be on the track. They could be goals for education, for travel, for career, or for family. But when a disproportionate amount of time and energy and money are poured into their appearance, it's easy to lose sight of what's most important.

I've also known girls who've gotten distracted when something gets too difficult. Maybe a girl started the volleyball or basketball or soccer season strong, but when training gets tough, she wants to quit.

If you start something, finish it. And finish strong! When you stick it out, when you push beyond adversity, you discover something in yourself that you didn't know you had. Until you give something 100 percent—whether it's guitar or tennis or Habitat for Humanity or surfing—you don't know what you're capable of achieving.

The year I broke the U.S. women's 400 record, I'd run fourteen other races. If I'd decided to take it easy after the fifth race, or tenth race, or twelfth, and just coasted through the rest of the season, I never would have achieved my dream. It wasn't until the fifteenth race that I broke the record!

Continue to believe in yourself no matter what distractions or obstacles you face.

Break It Down

To achieve your big goals, you need to avoid distraction by keeping your eyes on the finish line. That's the important lesson my father taught me.

But I also want you to know that the other secret to achieving your *big* goal is by making and achieving *smaller* goals. That's going to look different for every person, depending on what your goals are.

If you've set your mind on earning a full-ride scholarship to college, you might challenge yourself, one semester at a time, to get an A in every one of your classes. Perhaps you'll set your goal at 96 percent, or you might have your hands full aiming for 90 percent.

If you want to be the forward who makes 1,000 points during your high school basketball career, you might set a goal of making 24 points per game. And then put in the hours at the gym, at the park, and in your driveway practicing your shot!

If you want to raise enough money to fund a family-style orphan home in Haiti, you might decide to organize a fundraiser that will earn your first $5,000.

Breaking your big goal down into smaller goals can keep you motivated to reach the finish line and accomplish all you were made for.

And with every step, keep your eyes on the prize.

RIGHT ON TRACK CHALLENGE

It's easy to get distracted from the goals that are most important to you. You can stay focused by keeping your eyes focused on the finish line.

- What's one goal you're holding in your heart right now?
- What factors in your life have the most potential to distract you?

- What smaller goals do you need to set to reach your big one?
- What practical steps will keep you on track?

It's not unusual to get distracted during the race you're running. What is one thing you can do today to stay focused on achieving your dream?

CHAPTER 9

THE NUMBER ONE FAN OF
MY NUMBER ONE FAN

J ust give me a few weeks. She'll be my girl."
Those were the words my future groom spoke to
his mother as he pointed toward me from the University
of Texas bleachers. They were watching the Texas Relays,
a meet hosted by the University of Texas, and I was doing a
warm-up lap. I was sporting our signature burnt orange-and-
white uniform and my usual confident smile.

It took him more than a few weeks.

In fact, a year later, I was the one to make the first move!

I was having lunch with my sister in a campus cafeteria
when I spotted him. His name was Aaron Ross, but all his
friends called him Ross. Feeling confident, I waved him over
and we started talking. That week, he invited me to dinner
on Saturday night and to church on Sunday morning.

That was my kind of date!

If he was trying to win my heart, he couldn't have been any
more strategic. He was exactly the kind of guy I was looking
for: close with his mother, a gentleman on a Saturday night
date, and a committed Christian. His values matched mine.

107

The priorities that knit our hearts together were faith, family, and fitness.

Faith, Family, and Fitness

The fitness value is pretty obvious. When we met, I was running for the Longhorns and Ross was a defensive back on their football team. If you've ever heard of *Friday Night Lights*, I don't need to tell you that football is a pretty big deal in Texas. The town portrayed in the TV show is fictional, but Texas football madness is not.

Ross grew up in Tyler, Texas, where he played football two years for John Tyler High School. He didn't start playing football until his sophomore year! He also played basketball and was a sprinter. He was recruited by the University of Texas Longhorns, where he won a National Championship and was also awarded the Jim Thorpe Award for being the nation's top collegiate defensive back.

When we met in 2003, my eyes were fixed on competing in the Olympics and Ross's gaze was set on the NFL. While it meant we both had full schedules, it was sort of a match made in heaven. I didn't have to worry about Ross tempting me with French fries. And when I hit the floor to do my 1,000 sit-ups each night, Ross wasn't out drinking with the guys or sitting on the couch watching Netflix. He was at my side, joining in on the sit-ups and helping me count. It was like a nerdy athlete date. I felt so blessed that Ross understood the discipline needed to be the best.

As we reached each professional goal we'd set, we were

there to encourage each other in workouts and competitions along the way.

We were also both committed to our faith.

As we got to know each other, I learned that faith had always been important to Ross. When I asked him how long he'd had a relationship with Christ, he playfully answered, "Right out of the womb!" His grandmother was always in church and he'd been growing in his faith as long as he could remember. I loved that he was a prayerful person too.

And, of course, we each valued our families. My family is everything to me, and the same holds true for Ross. He's really close to his brother and sister, and he is absolutely devoted to his mother. (I'm not going to say that he's a momma's boy, but he does love his momma. Honestly, that was one of the first things I appreciated about him!) As I considered my dreams for the future, which included being married one day and having children, Ross was exactly the kind of man with whom I'd want to raise children.

I secretly hoped he felt the same.

Dating

Before you date, and while you date, one of the most important things I can encourage you to do is to know who you are. I remember clearly, from high school, the temptation to get all caught up in a boy: his likes, his friends, his wants, his needs. I saw a number of friends make those kinds of choices, and it never ended well. In an event at the Apollo Theater a few years ago, Michelle Obama offered girls advice about reaching their goals. She also warned against letting boys determine a girl's future. She herself was working as an associate at a Chicago law firm, focusing on her own dreams and ambitions, when she met her future husband, an intern at the firm!

If you're not yet dating, spend some time discovering who you are. Decide what goals you want to pursue and do what it takes to reach them. This is the time for you to become the best version of yourself.

If you are dating, take it slow. It's worth spending the time to really get to know somebody. And learn how to be yourself—who you really are—in that relationship. Don't feel pressured, by friends or by the person you're dating, to do anything you don't feel comfortable doing.

In fact, the best advice I can give you—whether you're dating or not yet dating—is to be yourself. A lot of times people can show a perfect, shiny side of themselves at the beginning of a relationship, but your bond will be much stronger if you're willing to let others see who you truly are. Maybe you're really goofy. Maybe you're awkward. Maybe you're quirky. Maybe you're bold. If you're willing to be who you are deep inside, you're going to be all right whether you're dating or not. Focus on who you were made to be and let God take care of the rest.

Two Surprises

It didn't take long for Ross and me to know we wanted to spend our lives together.

One of our favorite television shows to watch together was the comedy *Martin*. In the episode where Martin proposed to his sweetheart, Gina, his proposal was recorded.

So I wanted *my* proposal recorded!

During the year leading up to the 2008 Olympic games, NBC was filming profiles of various athletes. I was in New York for one of Ross's games, and the film crew was interviewing me.

Since we were both elite athletes, the network thought it would be interesting to film me getting ready, and then they'd also film me at the game.

Before Ross had to leave for the stadium, we were both sitting at the counter casually chatting. Well, as casual as you can be while cameras are rolling, anyway!

In a playful tone, he asked, "What do you want for Christmas?"

He knew exactly what I wanted. I wanted to be engaged.

"Babe . . ." I answered, unsure if I wanted everyone who'd be watching the Olympics to know I was ready for him to propose. I wanted to keep some things personal. I also didn't want to put him on the spot.

"Come on," he teased, "what do you *really* want?"

"What do I really want?" I asked, still deciding how much I was comfortable revealing.

Since he was pushing, I figured it wouldn't bother him if I said it.

"A ring!" I burst out, with a little giggle.

He'd already given me a promise ring that I wore on my

right ring finger, signaling the direction in which we were headed.

"I gave you a ring," he said with a grin.

Glancing down, matching his mood, I countered, "Not *this* ring . . ."

With a twinkle in his eye, he opened his hand to show me a gorgeous diamond-studded engagement ring.

Coyly, he said, "What about this one?"

When I saw it, I started screaming.

He asked, "Is that a yes?"

"YES!!!!!"

Yes. Yes. Yes.

When we'd been dating at the University of Texas, Ross had wanted to buy me the perfect ring. But, like most college students, that meant waiting. His NFL contract meant he could finally buy me a ring he knew I'd love.

One of the coolest parts of that day was that the rest of my family was downstairs when he proposed. My sister had already seen the ring, but I ran downstairs to show it to my parents and celebrate with all of them.

When my parents, Shari, and I left for the game that evening, I still felt a warm glow inside—enough to insulate me from their jokes about not wearing my gloves in the bitter cold! They all knew there was no way I was covering my left hand at this game.

I relished being Ross's biggest fan, especially on that night! In the first half of the game he had a great play, intercepting a pass by the Redskins' quarterback. When I glanced up at the Jumbotron to see the replay of the pass interference, I was shocked to see a very different replay. Rather than seeing my fiancé's amazing interception, I—and eighty thousand of my closest friends—was watching Ross's proposal from earlier in the day!

It was awesome.

Way better than Martin and Gina.

Warnings

Before Ross and I were engaged, certain friends and family warned me that Ross would lose interest because I was pursuing a career that required a heavy time commitment. They cautioned that girls who dreamed of sitting in the wives' suite on NFL Sundays would be lining up to steal him.

I understood their concerns.

There is no shortage of women throwing themselves at professional male athletes. And the stereotype of the NFL wife—that I'd just signed on to be!—was a woman who'd be constantly at his side, glimmering like a Heisman trophy, and spending his millions on diamonds and clothes.

That stereotype didn't fit Ross, though. It wasn't what he valued. He was more interested in having a strong partner, one who'd pursue her own dreams and challenge him to meet his, than he was in a woman who smiled quietly at his side. Our relationship wasn't going to be derailed by girls waiting outside the locker room.

Still, the people who were warning me had seen plenty of stories like mine that didn't end well. Players who'd pledged their allegiance to a girlfriend, fiancée, or wife would rationalize being with other women out on the road. Some of the strongest ones compromised their own values in the face of temptation.

Those were the kinds of thoughts that triggered my own insecurities. Was I present enough? Was I beautiful enough? Was I supportive enough? Was I *enough*? My worries, of course, had nothing to do with Ross. They were the unfortunate intersection of NFL culture and a strong, successful woman with a soft heart who, in the end, had the same tender spots as any other woman.

In my worst moments, my mind would play nasty tricks. When we were in college, a teammate had gossiped to me that she'd seen another girl driving Ross's car three days earlier. I freaked out until I did the math and realized Ross had come over to my apartment for dinner that night! His car had been parked outside my place the whole evening.

Thankfully, the fears that seemed like ominous warnings at the time proved to be unfounded. Our rigorous training and travel schedules only made us more grateful for the time we had together.

Finish Line or Starting Blocks?

After being engaged for more than two years, we married on February 26, 2010.

Walking down the aisle, supported by our families and friends and coaches, felt surreal. After dating for five years, we'd finally reached the finish line. We both felt like we'd won the prize! But, of course, the wedding also felt like being poised in the starting blocks, ready to begin our journey through life together.

As the wedding began, my dad escorted me to the back of the church. My dress was covered with gold and silver beading. It had a long train covered with crystals that shimmered as I walked. My hair fell in soft curls. Because the ceremony was being recorded for an episode of *Platinum Weddings*, a jeweler had loaned me $500,000 worth of jewelry to wear that day. (Yikes!)

I looked down the aisle and spotted Ross, calm and strong, wearing a white tuxedo. I felt like I was seeing my prince and I was his princess. I was glad I had my dad to lean on as I walked down the aisle. Before my dad released me to my beloved, he lifted my veil and kissed my cheek.

While a lot of that day was a blur, I knew one thing for sure: Ross and I were meant for each other. Standing before God, family, and friends, we pledged ourselves to one another for life.

Finding Balance

When it comes to pursuing your purpose, women can be faced with some unique challenges. Balancing our relationships with the sense of purpose God has given us takes thought and prayer.

For instance, when men reach for their dreams, personally or professionally, no one warns them that they might lose their girlfriends, fiancées, or wives! In fact, setting and reaching goals makes a man more desirable in the eyes of most, not less desirable. Still, finding the balance that's right can be a challenge. Most young women I know have dreams they want to accomplish, and many also look forward to being married and having children one day.

The problem I've seen is when women abandon who they are in order to get a man. I've seen girls bail on their friends the second a guy shows interest. I've seen girls date guy after guy after guy, in the hopes that the next one will be "the one." And I've also seen girls throw themselves at guys—like the NFL groupies!—in the hopes that one will pay attention to them and value them.

Believe this: women always lose when they sacrifice who they are for a guy.

The strongest women I know are ones who are solidly rooted in the reality that they are enough because they're loved by God. That foundation is what helps them navigate all the complicated questions about how to balance work and relationships.

I've had to navigate some of these same issues in our relationship. I loved Ross more than anything and wanted to be there to support him. At the same time, I wanted to accomplish the goals I'd set for myself. Even when naysayers were whispering warnings, I knew that my passion and drive to excel in my sport was something that God had knit into me, and it was also something that Ross loved about me. It's not like he'd spotted me in home ec class and fallen in love with my tacos! (We always joke about this because his mom makes a mean taco.) The day he pointed me out to his mom, I was in my element. I was confident, assured, ready to race. That's who he fell in love with, and that's who he chose to marry. He doesn't need me to be someone I'm not, trying to please him. I'm the best wife to Ross when I'm being who I really am. I know it and he knows it.

Every day Ross let me know that I was his one true love and that he was mine. This foundation was stronger than either one of us individually. We prayed together before every one of my races and we asked God to help us run the race he had for us as a couple. And, honestly, that's the reason I knew I never had to worry about another person interfering with our relationship. Our faith was always the foundation to move forward together as husband and wife.

If you think about the possibility of marriage in your future, choose someone who shares your faith commitments. You don't have to be on the same page about everything, but you do need to be on the same page about faith. Ultimately, marriage is about three people: your beloved, God, and you. Keep God at the center of your marriage and it will thrive.

One of the biggest reasons that's so important is because marriage is a lifelong commitment between two imperfect people. That's no small thing. I've known girls who wanted to believe that marriage would change the imperfect guy they married. Unfortunately, it doesn't work that way. Yes, people change. But you can't expect that marriage is going to "fix" anything. We can be tempted to convinced ourselves that "he'll settle down," or "he'll be kinder," or "he'll be different when he has a ring." Probably not. That's why you need to find someone who's solid and who's going to join you in keeping God in the center of your marriage.

Maybe someone a bit like my Ross.

RIGHT ON TRACK CHALLENGE

What are you looking for in someone you date or marry?

- Do you want God to be at the center of your relationship?
- What values or qualities are non-negotiable for you?
- What are the goals you'll be pursuing that aren't up for grabs?
- Who can help you stay true to who you really are?

Don't let your dating life happen in isolation. Choose a friend, relative, or mentor you value to walk that journey with you. Tell her now what matters most to you.

CHAPTER 10

BODIES IN MOTION

B eing invited to Nike headquarters in Beaverton, Oregon, for a photo shoot for its latest product line should have rocked my world.

A lot of people never consider how professional track and field athletes make a living. Prize money is awarded for winning races, but the awards are modest. And, they're only available during competition season. In a career that has a very short window of opportunity, endorsements from corporate sponsors are one of the ways we pay the bills. Since the first day of my professional career, I'd been sponsored by Nike, a brand I love.

When Nike invited me to do a photo shoot, I was thrilled to say yes. But the week I traveled to Oregon, I was glad my mom was going with me, because I was feeling terribly nervous about my appearance.

I wasn't concerned about looking fat. I'd been doing daily workouts that burned about 5,000 calories since I was young! In fact, I took for granted the confidence that came from having a sculpted body. I was used to people remarking how toned my arms were, how they envied my legs, and how they'd die for my six-pack. *Fit* was just my normal. I never thought twice about it.

But as our flight landed in Portland, I noticed that I was keenly connected to the kind of body shame so many women deal with every day.

A Painful Development

About six months earlier, a contract I had with AT&T gave me the opportunity to film a commercial at my home, alongside NFL legend Deion Sanders. I was twenty-five years old. I was really looking forward to it—both working with Deion and having the opportunity to connect with more fans.

Weirdly, though, about a week before we were scheduled to film, I developed mouth ulcers—frightening white pustules—that were so painful I couldn't talk or even take a sip of water without pain. My doctor gave me an ointment to use, as well as one for a lesion I'd noticed on my chest, and for a short time I experienced some relief. But the night before Deion was scheduled to come to town, the ulcers were back with such a vengeance that I couldn't even open my mouth.

My mother was concerned and begged me to go to the emergency room for help, but I insisted on doing the shoot. Amazingly—maybe due to my adrenaline, determination, and excitement—I not only made it through the gig, I also had several pain-free days. But a week later the excruciating symptoms returned. In addition to the mouth ulcers, the lesions on my skin had spread beyond my chest to impact my arms, back, legs, and stomach. It looked like my skin was poisoned. I continued to apply the ointment I'd been given, but as soon as one sore resolved, another would appear. When I woke up in the mornings, my skin looked as though someone had burned me with an iron. The affected skin looked burnt, almost black. I felt hopeless and helpless.

It was a painful season that only my family and closest friends shared with me. As my skin was ravaged beyond my control, I felt scared. Lost. I didn't believe I could measure up to society's expectations for what a strong, athletic woman should look like.

It was a stressful season too. For every public appearance, my mom and I would strategically choose clothing that covered my ulcerated skin. We tediously applied makeup to camouflage any areas that were exposed. The hardest events, of course, were races.

For months after the shoot with Deion Sanders, I crisscrossed the country in search of a doctor who could tell me what germ or virus was causing me to look and feel the way I did. We finally found a doctor in New York who was able to diagnose my condition as Behçet's disease. Behçet's is a rare autoimmune disorder, but no specific cause has been established. Though it is not contagious, it appears most frequently in the eastern Mediterranean, Middle East, and East Asia areas.

To this day, I still have no idea how I'd contracted Behçet's. It's a hereditary disease, but no one in my family had it and no one I spoke to in Jamaica had even heard of it.

And although the disease still felt scary and confusing, I

was relieved to have a diagnosis and a roadmap for treatment. Medication made it manageable at times, but I still continued to suffer with the symptoms.

Arriving at Nike

Nike had sent a car to pick up my mom and me from the airport. I continued to worry about how the day might unfold on the way to headquarters.

Because I'd done photo shoots with Nike before, I knew what to expect. I'd be wearing their newest gear designed for athletes. While the shoes and sports bras and Lycra shorts are functional for sport, they leave little to the imagination. There would be a lot of skin showing. My skin.

Until that moment, my family had seen the ravaging effects of my condition, but I hadn't needed to face much public scrutiny. When my mom and I were escorted into the studio, it was as I'd expected: filled with photographers, lighting assistants, and others who would facilitate the shoot.

My mom joined me in a changing booth as I stripped out of the clothes I'd worn on the airplane. She and I had both mastered how to use makeup and clothing to disguise my scars and lesions. But I'd grown weary of hiding.

"Mom," I sighed, "I didn't do this to myself. I'm tired of hiding it."

She listened patiently.

I announced, "I'm going to embrace my reality."

I thought she might resist, but instead, she surprised me. "Go for it, baby girl."

Her support meant the world to me and gave me the courage to step out of that dressing room and face a roomful of eyes who were used to viewing the perfect bodies of elite athletes. I was wearing a sleeveless cropped shirt and short Lycra tights.

The setup that day was epic. The room had been carefully staged with lights and backdrops. People were dashing in every direction. It felt like an honor and a privilege, but I noticed a now-familiar knot in my stomach.

As I walked toward the center of the room from the dressing room, I felt the eyes of others following me. Though I'd brought makeup, I'd not yet applied it to my stomach, back, legs, and arms. I noticed that some folks turned away quickly, being careful not to stare.

As the group began to gather around me, I smiled. "Guys, I have an autoimmune disease. It scars my skin, but it is not contagious and I'm fine."

I could read the relief on their faces and I felt the tension in the room dissipate.

I realized, in that moment, I was the one who could set the tone for others to know how to respond. And it worked! We had a fantastic shoot. It took courage to be uncovered in front of a group of people I didn't know, but I'm glad I did it. The photos turned out beautifully, as the post-production team smoothed all my scars for the campaign.

That experience changed me. It gave me such compassion for and an affinity with women and girls who struggle with a variety of issues related to appearance. Whether we struggle with weight, or with a skin discoloration, or disfigurement, or disability, or hair loss, or injury, just about every woman and girl knows what it is to feel as though we fall short of society's expectations.

And though I'd never fully noticed the ways those messages were being communicated before, I suddenly began to see and hear them everywhere: television, magazines, videos, online ads. The way those expectations were conveyed were never explicit. Not once did I hear anyone say, "You need to look like a flawless Barbie doll." But I began to notice the way that very message saturated both the media and women's psyches.

Some thought their skin tone was too dark.

Some wanted to be thinner or more toned.

Others desperately wanted their hair to be different than it was.

And others wanted to be taller or shorter.

I'll confess that the thoughts I'd have about my body were always an odd juxtaposition. On one hand, it was this amazing body that was faster than any other woman's body in the country! When I ran, my body was doing exactly what God designed mine to do. And that was amazing. But when it came to my skin, I was often filled with shame over how my body appeared to others.

Whenever I was tempted to despair, I remembered what my body could do and reminded myself: *God made my body good.*

Attempted Fixes

One day I had an idea about how I could fix the discoloration the scarring was causing in my skin.

Because I'm naturally brown-skinned, I'd never gone to a sunless tanning booth before, but this seemed like it might help even out my skin tone. Though I believe that there are ways for folks with brown skin to achieve a natural-looking color in a tanning booth, that was not my experience. There were different shades of spray, but I needed the most extreme one because of the darkness of the lesions. I got sprayed and then was put into an oven-like machine to bake, so that the coloring would "set" and not rub off on the inside of clothing.

Let's just say that when I'd finished baking, I was not any kind of color that was recognizably human. You know how the Oompa Loompas in *Charlie and the Chocolate Factory* were pretty orange? I wasn't orange, but I was so darkly discolored that I also was unrecognizable!

I think it's fair to say that the tanning salon was not the best option for me.

A better fix did come along, though, right when I needed it most.

Not long after we'd visited Nike's headquarters, I was having a really bad outbreak on my arms. One afternoon I received a box in the mail of the newest line of running wear. My mom, who is usually as excited as I am to see what comes from Nike, opened the box for me.

I saw her staring at what was inside and shaking her head.

When I went over to look at what they'd sent, she announced, "God is so good to you."

Nike's newest style for female runners was compressed arm sleeves!

They'd been in development too long to have been created in response to the photo shoot of my less-than-perfect skin, but it did feel like a gracious gift from above.

My silent prayers had been heard.

Getting Over It

I couldn't wear arm sleeves everywhere, though. And although Photoshopping my skin for the Nike campaign was a success, digitally altering my image was less feasible when I wasn't being viewed in a print ad.

In the spring of 2011, Ross and I were headed to a track meet held annually in Austin called the Texas Relays. It was mainly for high school and college kids, but a few pros competed there. When we arrived, it was scorching hot. Well over 100 degrees.

Any other year I could have worn long sleeves to the event. But with the blazing heat that year, I would have looked and felt ridiculous.

The morning of the event, I stared into my closet. This wouldn't be like Nike: a studio of thirty people I could explain Behçet's to. There would be thirty thousand track fans at the Relays. Ross and I were going that day as spectators.

"Babe," I said to Ross, who was also getting ready, "what should I wear?"

He'd never found my skin condition to be as distracting as I did. In fact, seeing no reason to be ashamed of it, he'd always encouraged me to embrace everything about my appearance. I knew he'd have my back.

I chose a white sleeveless shirt and jeans. Though I was used to wearing very little fabric on my body, I felt as exposed as most women do in a string bikini at the beach!

When we arrived at the race, fans began to come up to us and ask for autographs and selfies together. Always grateful for the affection of my awesome fans, I was happy to oblige.

"Babe," Ross whispered in my ear, "most people aren't even seeing it. You're fine. It's all in your head."

And he was right.

What felt like a hideous distraction to me was barely noticeable to others.

When I peeked on Facebook that night, I could see that in some of the pictures it looked like I was cringing. Oh well, I was proud of myself for letting go of my insecurities and facing the world.

Glancing over my shoulder at my iPad, Ross whispered again, "Baby, you're beautiful."

That day, his voice sounded a lot like the voice of the One who made me.

Getting Comfortable in This Skin

I want you to hear that although I believe with all of my heart that God made our bodies good, and doesn't want us to undergo the shame that harms us, I didn't experience a sudden magical moment when I could look at the parts of me I didn't like and immediately feel great about myself.

It took time.

Initially, I was tremendously insecure. It was hard for me to find inner confidence and peace. In the beginning, I *did* wear long sleeves in 110-degree heat!

For a while, my assumptions and preconceived ideas about who I was needed to catch up with the truth about who God had determined I was. Each day I was able to agree with what was true, I experienced more and more freedom.

I'm not defined by this condition.

I didn't do anything to deserve this condition.

The judgment of those who don't understand this condition doesn't affect me.

It took me years of clinging to those truths to become comfortable in my scarred skin.

A few years ago, my dermatologist suggested that I wean off the drugs I'd been taking for Behçet's and instead pay close attention to relieving some of the stressors in my life. Really? The prescription I was receiving was to take long baths and relax? I could do that!

My favorite relaxation day started with a long hot bath while watching *The Golden Girls*. (If you don't know the silly sitcom from the late '80s and early '90s, promise me you'll google it.) It was light and funny and allowed me to laugh. Then I'd read. Some of my favorite books included Joyce Meyer's *Battlefield of the Mind* and Devon Franklin's *Produced by Faith*. I always love hearing how other people made it through difficult times, and those books really inspired me. Don't get me wrong, my training was still intense, so every moment wasn't a hot bubble bath! But I was able to treat my nervous system with kindness and TLC.

Though I sometimes will experience a recurrence of mouth ulcers, I don't experience the same global outbreaks I once did. When I don't wear makeup, you can even recognize a little black scar on the corner of my mouth—my war wounds.

It reminds me of the battle I once fought daily.

And it reminds me how far I've come.

Today I have an inner confidence and strength that no one can take away from me. I can enjoy a glamorous day of getting beautiful for a special event, or I can kick around the house in sweats and no makeup. I've learned how to value who I am above what I look like and, of course, to value others that way too.

Change It or Love It

If there's something you'd like to be different about your body, I encourage you to do one of two things.

If it's something you can change by honoring your body and treating it right, with healthy diet and exercise, then go for it. And practice patience. Getting healthy isn't something that happens overnight. It takes time, so be patient with yourself.

But in a lot of cases—if you don't like your eyes or your ears, if you think your hips are too wide or your legs are too thin—the biggest win may be to simply choose to be satisfied with who you are and how you look. That choice is one that blesses you and blesses those around you. Believe me, I know it's not always easy. It took me three years to wear a sleeveless shirt in public! I get it. But learning to be comfortable in your own skin—no matter the color, shape, or texture—is what you're made for.

I've often noticed that the women who have the prettiest spirits, the ones who radiate beauty from the inside, are the ones who, regardless of their physical features, seem the most attractive to others. Although our culture tells us that beauty comes from something outside of us—the curve of a nose, the shine of our hair, the products we use, the outfits we buy—I believe we cultivate beauty by tending to what's on the inside. In my opinion, that's good news, because true beauty doesn't have to depend on either good genes or a lot of money to buy good jeans! As you feed your spirit by welcoming God to transform you, by spending time with other believers, by tipping your face toward God's word and God's voice, you nurture a beauty that can never fade. You invest in beauty that lasts.

If you decide to embrace the goodness of accepting yourself as you are, I encourage you to notice the women around you who embody that freedom already. Who's a woman you know—in your family, at your church, at your school, in your neighborhood—who is comfortable in her own skin? As you look around, I think you'll notice that these women come in a variety of sizes, shapes, colors, and personalities! Discover what it is that fuels this woman's confidence.

What is it about this woman that you admire? Does she spend more time noticing others than she does looking in the mirror? Does she have a faith in God that gives her a purpose that's grander than taking great selfies?

Learn from the women around you who are living in freedom.

Choosing to accept yourself as you are, and not as others might advise you to be, allows you to live in the freedom you're made for.

Trust me, it's the best way.

RIGHT ON TRACK CHALLENGE

Is there something about your body you'd like to change?

- Is there something you can change with healthy practices?
- Are you being called to embrace the way you're made?
- What does it look like to live in that freedom?
- What can you do today to choose freedom?

Talk to a woman who's comfortable in her own skin, and then journal about that encounter. Ask God to equip you to live into the freedom for which you're made.

CHAPTER 11

REACHING FOR YOUR GOALS

In the 2008 Summer Olympic Games in Beijing, I'd earned a bronze medal in the 400. While I could see how that was a huge accomplishment, I was disappointed by it. I'd come to win, and I wanted to go home with gold.

My teammates and I would have the opportunity to do it in the 4x400 relay.

Mary Wineberg, Allyson Felix, Monique Henderson, and I made it to the finals and were placed in lane 4, beside Russia, our greatest rivals outside of Jamaicans.

Monique ran the third leg. When she handed me the baton, we were in second place. I knew that many runners faced the temptation to power ahead of the competition with a burst of speed too soon. And while it would have been great to take the lead early, I knew I wanted to save something for the home stretch so I had the lead when it counted. I chose to run my own race, the one Coach Clyde and I had agreed on, and my goal for the first half of the lap was to not let Anastasiya Kapachinskaya get too far away from me.

With sixty meters left in the race, I decided I was going for the gold. (I know it's a cliché, but that moment—and all that it meant to me, to my teammates, and my country—is why the cliché even exists!) I made my move, pulling out of the inside lane into the second lane, accelerating and passing Kapachinskaya. In the last ten meters, feeling the strength of my legs beneath me, I knew I had the win. I thrust my upper body across the finish line, pumping the baton in the air as I crossed. That finish has been called one of the most thrilling gold medal moments in the Olympic Games. And not just by my parents! My teammates gathered around me, and we prayed right there on the track, thanking God for the privilege and strength to do what we'd been born and trained to do.

Glancing toward the stands, I located my mom, Shari, and the other family and friends who'd come to support me and the team. My mom was going wild! It was everything my whole family had worked so hard for. Though the medal would be draped around my neck, I knew I was holding it for all of us.

A Joyful Homecoming

The United States 2008 Summer Olympic team brought home 110 medals, more than any other country. It wasn't just women's track and field that were bringing home gold, either. Michael Phelps, Ryan Lochte, and the men's swim team were wearing them. Kristin Armstrong had one in cycling. Nastia Liukin and Shawn Johnson donned them for gymnastics. Venus and Serena Williams won gold for women's doubles tennis. Kerri Walsh Jennings and Misty May-Treanor grabbed gold in beach volleyball. Our women's and men's basketball teams—Lisa Leslie, LeBron, Kobe—all brought home gold.

Before we'd left Beijing, the entire U.S. Olympic team— 596 athletes—had been invited to appear on *The Oprah Winfrey Show* in Chicago. Not all of us showed up, but most of us did. As you might guess, we didn't fit in Oprah's studio.

The show to celebrate the returning American Olympians was filmed outside, on a stage constructed just for that episode. Our relay team was among the few teams Oprah had selected to interview. She was chatting with Nastia Liukin and Shawn Johnson right before our segment. Shawn had won gold in women's balance beam, and she and Nastia had competed head to head in the women's artistic individual all-around, with Nastia surprising many by winning the gold. Because we were scheduled to be interviewed next, the four of us were close enough to hear that interview.

When Oprah asked Nastia the secret to her success, Nastia mentioned her father's influence and also said that creating a vision board had been crucial to her victory.

My ears perked up.

She'd created a vision board that showed all she hoped to achieve. It included pictures from magazines, competitions, medals, and scores. She said that being able to visualize her goals helped her accomplish them.

Completely smitten by the idea, I thought, *I'm totally going to do that.*

I've always been a visual person. In high school, I'd begun taping my goals to the mirror in my bedroom, and

I always kept journals where I recorded my times and set goals for future times and records I intended to break. So when I heard that creating a vision board had been helpful for Nastia, something clicked, and I immediately knew that I'd be implementing the practice.

I created my first vision board in 2009. Just the process of putting it together helped me think through what I wanted to accomplish. And once I hung it on the wall, where I could see it every day, I was forced to ask myself: *How will I get there?* Once I decided I wanted to win individual Olympic gold, write a book, and start a business, the vision board helped me to see not only the process I'd need to embrace, but also the partners who'd help me get there.

Achieving your dreams requires envisioning the end result.

Whether it's the goals you have for yourself as a Christian, as a student, as an athlete, or as an artist, being able to see where you're headed is critical. If you can't picture where you're going, chances are you'll never arrive.

Once you see the end game, though, you can develop a plan to get there.

While many of my own goals have been on the track, the dreams and goals you have for your life may happen in other arenas. Maybe you want to start a band. Perhaps there's a dream job you'd love to do when you're older. Maybe you want to create and sell your artwork. Or you might want to get a graduate degree. When you can see where you eventually want to be—crossing a finish line, on stage at Madison

Square Garden, counseling foster children, being featured in a prominent art gallery, or teaching undergrads—you can craft a plan to get there.

First, though, you need to see it.

Shari's Dream

Because my family has been such a huge support to me throughout my athletic career, and because my sister Shari has been my biggest fan, some people have wondered whether she got lost in my shadow.

Nothing could be further from the truth.

Shari never wanted to be like me. She always had her own identity, and she was passionate about finding her own thing.

After a few semesters in college, Shari realized that a four-year degree might not be the path to reach her goals. She was passionate about hair and wanted to attend cosmetology school. Traditional education, however, was a really big deal in our family. It's why my parents had wanted us to move to America in the first place: we'd have opportunities to attend great schools and win meaningful scholarships. So when Shari first told our parents she wanted to go to cosmetology school, they resisted. They wanted her to stay in college.

Never one to stay silent, I went to bat for my best friend at the dinner table one evening after I'd gone pro.

"But *I* left school early," I reminded our mom and dad.

"But that's—" my dad began, prepared to say how my situation was different.

I cut him off. "No, it's not different. If she has found

something she loves, the way I love running, why shouldn't she have the same opportunity to pursue her passion?"

It took more than one dinner to convince them, but eventually our folks conceded that we were right.

If I can use the cliché, Shari went for her gold.

She sought out individuals who were doing celebrity hair, or those who'd started their own businesses, and built relationships with them to learn whatever they could teach her. She earned her cosmetology license. She took classes all over the country to gain expertise in her craft. She took cutting classes in New Orleans. She attended coloring classes in Los Angeles. She pursued excellence with a passion. Though I don't think she had a vision board, she had a picture in her mind of that finish line: owning and operating a successful salon. And because she could see the finish line, she crafted and executed the plan that would help her get there. Today, Shari owns a salon.

I am so proud of my sister. And I want you to hear that achieving your goals begins with being able to see them and enacting a plan to get there.

Seeing the Finish Line

Even though I didn't have a vision board in high school, I can look back now at the ways I envisioned my goals and implemented plans to reach them.

When I was in middle school, I knew I wanted to win at the county championships. So I wrote, "Win the 100 at County Championships" on a notecard and taped it to my mirror. Though I didn't know it at the time, experts say that posting a goal in place where you can see it regularly increases the odds of achieving it.

For as long as I can remember, I've also recorded my goals in a journal.

Initially, I'd choose a cute one from the local Christian bookstore. I'd usually get soft padded ones with inspirational messages on the cover and the inside pages. Under the Scriptures at the top of the page, I'd write about my day, what was happening in my family, my classes, my meets, as well as my thoughts. In my journal, I had a friend on the journey. In fact, when I finally met my own personal goal in high school for the 400, I dished to my journal, "You won't believe it! I ran the 400 in 50.6!" I almost expected applause from my paper companion!

Eventually my cousin Shelley began buying me a journal every year for Christmas. One of those journals, by a black artist, read, "Be Your Own Boss." Shelley had inscribed it, "Here's to you fulfilling all your dreams. Love you, Shelz."

Beyond the typical pages where I wrote about what I did during the day, or what boy I was crushing on, I'd also chronicle my workouts. Since I'd do the same routine every Monday, Tuesday, etc., I'd write down my times, noting if I was slower or faster than the previous week. I'd also note if the workout felt easier or more difficult. That process—reviewing where I'd been, noticing where I was, and planning for where I'd be in the future—was a great way to hold myself accountable to reaching the goals I'd taped on my mirror.

Hayward Field

When I was seventeen, I reached my goal of setting a new Florida state record when I ran the 400 for my high school in 52.51.

That night, I wrote in my journal, "The next record to break is the national record of 50.74." In fat Sharpie marker, I wrote "50.73" on an index card and carefully taped it to my mirror.

Several weeks later, I had the rare opportunity of attending the highly select Prefontaine Classic meet. This meet held every spring in Eugene, Oregon, featured the top track and field athletes from all over the world. A high school athlete was invited to the event only every five years or so, and that year—as the person who'd run the fastest girls' 400 time in the nation—I was the only one to receive an invitation.

My dad and I flew to Eugene together, and it was so great to have him there for support. Since grade school, my dad had been filming each of my races so that we could review them the evening of the meet. We'd watch each race six or seven times. The first several times he'd point out everything I was doing right: my start, my posture, my stride, my arms. Then, eventually, we'd search for ways I could improve my race to cut my time. Because the Prefontaine was being broadcasted by ESPN2, it was the first meet that my dad didn't have to film!

Competing in the Prefontaine was huge for me. It was a meet I'd dreamed of competing in after college, and I'd made it there as a teenager. As I was warming up, I realized I was running with amazing athletes like Gail Devers, Stacy Dragila, and Marion Jones.

No pressure, right?

In that pack of world-class professional runners, I wasn't predicted to do any better than finish last. I understood that. But in my heart of hearts, I secretly wanted to dazzle the world. What kept me grounded and motivated to do my best was keeping my eye on the national junior record—50.74—then held by Monique Henderson. The same Monique I'd go on to share gold with in Beijing!

In the end, I missed the national junior record. But I did surprise everyone with a second-place finish. What felt absurd—particularly for a Jamaican who'd been raised to believe that second place was first loser!—was that the announcer called me back on the track after the finish to run a victory lap. The crowd at Hayward Field, some of the most knowledgeable and appreciative track fans in the world, stood and applauded for me for finishing second! Only in America.

As my dad and I flew back to Miami, I knew that the national high school record of 50.74 would be waiting for me.

It was on my bedroom mirror.

Eyes on the Prize

In high school, AP Calculus was kicking my rear. There was this really nice, smart kid in my class named Vic. He and I had several honor and AP classes together and I decided, "If Vic can get an A, then I can get an A." Yes, I had a bit of a competitive streak! Vic was my friend and keeping up with him inspired me to do my best. Calculus, though, was harder for me than a sprint.

Whether you're trailing in the 4x400 on the international stage or trailing in Calc, sometimes you've just got to make up your mind that you're going to win.

Vic was my competition, but—like DeeDee Trotter or Natasha Hastings, American teammates I competed against to become my best—he was also a teammate. So after class each day, during our lunch hour, Vic and I would go over any of the concepts I didn't understand. Isn't that cool?

Over the years I've tried to be that kind of a teammate to others—one who helps them see their goals and reach them.

In addition to my goal to get a 4.0 grade point average, and be invited to join the National Honor Society, I was still working my plan to become the runner who would break the national record.

In order to improve my core strength, I started doing one thousand sit-ups every day. The full routine took about an hour, so I carved out windows of time throughout the day to get in one hundred or two hundred sit-ups so I had completed my one thousand before bedtime. Most often I'd knock them out at track practice or later at home. My dad was still playing soccer for a minor league team in Florida, and when he was home he'd often do my workouts with me while my mom counted for us.

One day my Economics teacher, Mr. Williams, was late for class. When he arrived, I was in the back of the class, on my back on the floor, doing as many sit-ups as I could before class.

"Sanya," he asked, "what are you doing?"

"I told you," I explained, "I'm trying to get ahead. Strengthening my core. Doing a thousand sit-ups a day."

"Really?" he queried. Then, wondering to himself if I'd get the same value and impact from doing five hundred sit-ups as I would from doing one thousand, he asked, "But isn't there a point of diminishing return?"

Econ teacher reasoning.

But when it came to my training, I believed I benefitted as much from my commitment to doing more than everyone else as I did from the exercise.

I stayed with one thousand.

Keep Your Eyes Open

Are you able to see the finish line?

If you can see your own finish line, find a way to keep it before your eyes. Maybe you'll choose to journal or create a vision board. Maybe you'll draft a goal card every year on January 1 that you review each year on December 31. Or maybe you'll record a video of you dishing with your best friend about your aspirations. If you want to be America's Next Top Chef, maybe you'll hang a rubber chicken from your ceiling. Whatever you hope to achieve, visualize what achieving that dream will look like. By keeping the finish line in sight, you can execute your plan to achieve your dreams.

I know that everyone approaches their goals in different ways, but it's important to have a plan.

The goals you set will determine that plan.

RIGHT ON TRACK CHALLENGE

What's one goal you want to achieve this year? Over the next five years? Over the next twenty years? Choose one goal and find a way to capture it.

- Make a vision board.
- Film a video.
- Tape a goal to your mirror.
- Start a journal.

CHAPTER 12

THE POWER OF BELIEF

I was seventeen years old the first time I was invited to the Prefontaine Classic. Competing alongside professional athletes as a high school student, on the heels of breaking the Florida state girls record for the 400, had been thrilling. Although part of me was disappointed to miss out on a win, even I realized that a silver medal at the Prefontaine was still a pretty big deal.

In 2012, I was back at Hayward Field at the University of Oregon in Eugene. The meet, always a highlight for U.S. track and field fans, continued to hold a special place in my heart as well. Although athletes had been running for a few weeks prior, the meet that typically fell during the last week of May marked the official start of the season.

The indoor track season started each year in February. Although I hadn't run indoor track in 2010 or 2011, I did run indoor that year, winning my first world title in Istanbul in March. I'd started the year strong.

But right before the Prefontaine, I'd been defeated in Jamaica. Instead of working my four P's, getting off the blocks, and getting into my rhythm, I'd run the second hundred meters too fast. Novlene Williams-Mills and I were neck and neck for the last half of the race, and she beat me by one hundredth of a second.

The Prefontaine was the second race of the official outdoor season, and I arrived holding both my Istanbul victory and my Jamaican defeat in my heart and mind.

Windblown

The wind that year was as fierce as my competitors. Stepping onto the main track for the finals of the 400 in a lightweight Nike tank top and thin racing shorts, the wind was howling. I felt it tugging against the single braid falling down my back.

Inclement weather affects athletes in every outdoor sport. Football and soccer players learn to play in rain and mud. On sunny days, major league baseball players, who once wore eye black to decrease glare, now wear sunglasses. Golfers adjust their swing to accommodate a headwind.

Runners also face rain and sun and wind, but there's a particularly unique feature about the 400, as well as the 800 and other races that loop the full length of the track. At a single point on a golf course, a golfer evaluates the impact of wind on her game and adjusts her swing in one single direction accordingly. A 100-meter sprinter can take stock of the wind knowing that she'll be running one hundred meters *in a single direction*. If the wind is at her back or in her face, she adjusts for it. But any track athlete running at least four hundred meters will run with the wind for part of her race and against the wind for another part. Running 360 degrees means that, either at the beginning, in the middle, or at the end, a 400-meter sprinter will face a headwind.

As I found my place in lane 4, shaking out my muscles and keeping my blood flowing, the prayer of my heart was for the wind to stop for sixty seconds. Just sixty seconds.

I felt a huge gust of wind blow through the stadium. If it continued to rush in the same direction, the angle of the wind would benefit me for only about two seconds of the final turn, and would then be a battle for the rest of the race.

"Runners, take your marks . . ."

My mind and heart were heavy with the *meaning* of this race. Winning the world title in Istanbul had positioned me for a great year. But my loss in Jamaica had rattled me. I understood what I'd done wrong, but if I'd erred in Jamaica, maybe my race would fall apart here at Hayward Field as well.

Despite that conflict I carried, I had come here to win. And among those I trusted the most—Mom, Dad, Shari—I would have admitted that I wanted to do more than win. I wanted to run my personal best. If I could leave Jamaica in Jamaica, there was no good reason I couldn't.

Except . . . the wind.

The announcer boomed, "Get set . . ."

In that moment, a prayer of authority that seemed to come from within me and beyond me at the same time bubbled up from my heart and off my lips.

"Peace," I announced to the wind, "be still."

Because I'm not in the habit of commanding the elements,

I was as surprised as anyone that I'd had the audacity to take command over nature! But in that holy moment—like none other I've ever experienced in my life—I felt God's presence with me.

And all at once, I was keenly aware that the wind ceased.

I heard God whispering to my spirit, "I'm with you. Run on faith."

Almost the way a dream seems to collapse scenes into time, that short experience pulsed with the fullness of God.

Had I been praying in my bedroom, I would have savored it for an hour. But in the twinkle of an eye, the starting gun signaled the start of the race.

Bang!

Running My Race

With a quiet confidence I believe comes from God, I executed the 4 P's Coach Hart and I had agreed on. As every muscle did what it had been trained to do, I felt a remarkable peace in my spirit. In my mind. In my body. By the time I'd come off the first turn, I was so certain of God's presence with me that I was aware of little else.

Coming down the home stretch, I had every confidence I would be the first woman across the finish line. I felt like I was running the race of my life. If I hadn't learned—the hard way!—not to look at the clock, I surely would have peeked.

As I leaned into the finish line, slowing steadily and bending to catch my breath, I felt exhilarated.

I received the kind hug of congratulations from a

competitor, but my mind was distracted as I waited for the official time to be posted.

After several excruciating seconds, digital red lights blinked: 49.39. The fastest time in the world.

I was thrilled with the time. Locating my mom and dad and Shari in the stands, I found them hopping up and down pumping their fists.

What I could not know in that electrifying moment was that two months later, when I would race in the London Olympics, the time that would earn me a gold medal would be a fraction of a second slower than the race I'd just won in Eugene.

God and Winning

I want to be very clear about something. Although my faith has always been the most important priority in my life, I have never believed that God was a secret weapon to win races.

Before NFL games, a chaplain prays with each team that is hoping for victory. Atheist ice skaters beat Christian ones. And I wouldn't fool myself into believing that while I was experiencing such a powerful awareness of God's nearness with me on Hayward Field, other runners who tipped their hearts toward heaven weren't also met by God's faithful presence.

God is not a magic genie we can command with our wishes. And my faith in God's power and reliability have never been contingent on victory on the track.

I believe God guides me in everything I do. One of the

ways God does that is through the wisdom he places in my heart when it comes to the people I select to be in my life. My coach was a godly Christian man. In fact, I was surrounded by believers who understood that the journey, my journey, was greater than breaking records and wearing gold melted into prestigious medallions. I have always considered those friends and family members and supporters who shared my values to be one of God's greatest gifts in my life.

I've also always had an awareness that God would walk with me whether I won or lost. Not only was God's nearness not dependent on my performance, but I have seen the ways God would enter into victories and defeats, illnesses and injuries, challenges and blessings, using each one to cultivate my character.

In defeat, God would teach me about humility. In the face of challenges, God might teach me a new way of doing something. If I failed, God was with me as I reevaluated what had gone wrong. And I don't just mean on the track. God teaches me, disciplines me, and shapes me every single day in my relationships, in my work, and in my marriage. There's no area of my life from which God is absent.

Does God Care?

Because I do recognize God's presence with me and God's presence with my competitors, it grieves me when people say, "God doesn't care if you win or lose." Honestly, it really aggravates me!

The reason for my annoyance has nothing to do with

winning or losing. It has to do with those first three words: "God doesn't care." While I don't think God injects divine energy into a runner who didn't put in the training, I am convinced that *God does care*. Because God cares about me, and because God cares about you, God does care if I win or lose, and he cares if *you* win or lose. God cares about the things that I care about and you care about!

And because God cares about me, God's engagement with me doesn't end with the fist pump or the pat on the back. The same way my dad helps me learn from my mistakes on the track, God uses everything in my life—wins and losses, joys and sorrows—to shape me more and more into the image of his Son. I believe God wants to teach me to depend on him. To trust him. To thank him. I believe that God wants to form me into the kind of woman who loves her teammates and loves her competitors. I believe God wants to use all my experiences, on and off the track, so that I become a beautiful reflection of Jesus.

I don't think that God values us according to whether we win or lose, but I do think that God is attentive to every detail of our lives. If it matters to us, it *does* matter to God.

And because I matter to God, God matters to me. Having a personal relationship with my Maker, the Father of Jesus, is the most important thing in my life. And just like I make time for my relationship with my husband, family, and friends, I also put a priority on making time for my relationship with God. For me that means carving out time for prayer and spending time in God's Word.

But I don't believe that Christians were ever meant to keep our faith bottled up as a private commodity. I value the importance of fellowship with other believers. When I'm in Austin on Sundays, I'm at my church home with my church family. And my time spent with God, in conjunction with being among the body of Christ, is what fuels me to be God's woman in the world.

Responding to God's Nudge

One of the ways to stay connected when I'm on the road is through Bible study with other athletes. In one competition, a chaplain was leading us in what God's call to love others looks like in our lives.

Thinking how easy it is to love the folks who love me and are on "Team Sanya," I remarked, "It's easy to love our friends and support them, but the challenge is to love and support people who aren't our friends."

It was as if a light bulb came on in that room as we all realized that, as competitors, we have that opportunity more often than most! I wouldn't label my competitors as enemies, but there is definitely a tension that comes with wanting the same prize.

As we all began to chime in about what that looked like for each of us, an athlete about two years younger than me chimed in.

"Well, Sanya," she began, "I'll never forget tryouts for the U.S. Team."

I remembered them as well. I had made the team, as had

a few other girls in our Bible study circle that evening, but this girl had not.

She continued, "You came over to me and asked if you could pray with me."

I remembered that sad and happy moment.

She reflected, "I never forgot that. I'd felt so low, like the life had been drained from my body. That meant so much to me. I don't know if I ever told you that."

Another girl chimed in, "You did that with me too!"

I don't invite others to pray because I'm particularly strong or super-spiritual. I asked these girls to pray because I knew how disappointed they were and I didn't know what else to do. I just wanted them to know that they not only mattered to me, they mattered to God. He could do the rest.

While I believe God calls us to share our faith, it's really not my style to be preachy about it. I actually don't think it's God's style either. More often, I think, God quickens our hearts to engage with others in moments that are more genuine than quoting a verse at them or wagging our fingers. But it does take courage to say yes when God leads us to care for others or share with them in ways that take us outside our comfort zones. I always want to be the woman who says yes when God calls.

Counting the Cost

Recently, a friend and I were chatting, and she asked me what my faith has cost me. I thought it was a great question. And as I reflected on my journey, I realized that it has looked a little different in each season of my life.

In high school, it cost me a guy.

I had made a promise in church when I was thirteen. I'd promised myself, and promised God, that I wouldn't have sex in high school. There was a guy I really, *really* liked, and he was pressuring me to have sex. When I made it clear that wasn't going to happen, he chose not to date me. That deeply hurt.

What made the situation even more difficult was that a good friend of mine, who at one time had shared my moral convictions, had recently lost her virginity. It didn't change my conviction, but it muddied the waters. She'd compromised and gotten the guy. I'd remained true to what I believed and lost the guy. Though it was painful at the time, today I'm so glad I stood my ground. I don't regret it for a moment.

As I got older, sticking to my convictions didn't get any easier. One of my favorite teammates from the University of Texas and I were racing in Europe. Rassin and I had a down day in Paris, and had gone out to lunch with some runners from Eastern Europe. Rassin was telling us how she'd had a killer headache all day.

Another athlete reached into an unzipped pocket of her backpack and pulled out a little baggie filled with pills.

Holding out two pills in the palm of her hand, offering them to Rassin, she said, "Here, you can try these."

I read Rassin's face and realized that she might take them, as if they were aspirin, to be polite.

I whispered under my breath, "You can't take that! Don't take it."

Emboldened, she agreed.

"Thanks," she replied, "but I'm good."

We finished our lunch, but on our walk back to the hotel we wondered what the pills might have been. Though they didn't look to me like over-the-counter pain relievers, it's possible they were European aspirin! But I also knew that drugs have, unfortunately, been rampant—in various eras—in international track and field.

In a nutshell, performance-enhancing drugs are substances that boost athletic performance. They include steroids, human growth hormone, stimulants, and others. Most are illegal. For example, a drug used for "blood-doping" increases aerobic capacity by increasing red blood cells. It was banned by the International Olympic Commission in 1985, and made illegal in 1986, but has made a resurgence in recent years among both runners and cyclists. Too many athletes use that shortcut. It's been proven that a number of athletes who broke world records in the mid-eighties—some who've never been stripped of those titles—were abusing anabolic steroids. There was such a rapid drop in race times that even thirty years later we haven't caught up in many events!

I was never willing to compromise my values, or my integrity, for a win I didn't earn. And it makes me so angry that the sport I love has been tarnished by the abuse of drugs. God has designed human bodies to do amazing things. If you only turned on your television once every four years to peek at the Olympic games, you'd see a spectacular demonstration of what human beings are capable of achieving. I think it's remarkable, and I think that performing clean honors God as our good Creator.

Empowered

People who don't know me, who've only seen me race from the stands or on YouTube, don't know what propels me. When I pull ahead of the pack in the last fifty meters of a race, they assume it's because of my thick quads. Or a natural ability. They could chalk my achievements up to nature or training or even good luck.

But I know that I'm fueled by something more powerful than highly developed muscle tissue and good genes. Whether it's in a moment when the wind stands still, as it was in Eugene, or under the rigorous pressures of teen life or professional demands, my power, my motivation, my drive, and my integrity all come from God. He is the one who can say to my heart, in any situation, "Peace, be still."

RIGHT ON TRACK CHALLENGE

Is your faith empowering you to run your race well?

- Are you carving out time to spend in God's Word?
- Are you fellowshipping with other Christians?
- Are you setting aside quiet time to pray?
- Are you responding to God's voice in faithful obedience?

Whatever is important to you is important to God. If you want to deepen your relationship with him today, seek out someone you respect as a spiritual leader and share your heart.

_____

CHAPTER 13

SAILING OVER HURDLES

Do you want to be the best?"
  As I trace the long path to reaching my goals, searching for when it began, I think back to a conversation my dad and I had in high school. I can still see the look in my father's eyes and hear the serious tone of his voice. I remember him sitting across from me in our living room the summer before my senior year of high school.

When I failed to answer quickly, he asked again.

"Do you want to be the best?"

That season in my running journey was a pivotal one. I'd suffered from a hamstring injury my junior year and hadn't competed well at nationals. Until that point I'd been running and winning, but I wasn't working much harder than my teammates and competitors from other schools.

After the state finals that year I'd gone on to the Junior Olympics, where I'd finished fifth in the long jump and sixth in the hundred. My dad's poignant question, about whether or not I wanted to be the best, made me take ownership for my own performance.

After he asked, I never looked back.

On the heels of being injured, he helped me recognize

the difference between those who are good because of innate talent and those who put in the hard work to be great.

I wanted to be great.

Bad Toe

The large toe on my right foot began bothering me toward the end of the season during my junior year of high school. After some rest before the season revved up for senior year, I was feeling relief. But by the end of senior year, I was again experiencing a quiet, nagging pain.

Each year, the pain would return earlier and earlier in the season. By 2007, it had become a real problem. I'd made the world championship team, but my toe had really been bothering me during the four or five competitions leading up to it. And when I say four or five competitions, I mean every day, every warm up, every workout, every step. That small little digit caused a lot of trouble.

The joint at the base of the big toe is arguably the most important joint in the foot for running. So my parents scheduled appointments for me with the very best sports medicine doctors. I was diagnosed with hallux rigidus. It was a hereditary condition my mom also shared, but without the same constant wear and tear my toe was subjected to, hers had not gotten as bad as mine. If you think about the torque that's needed to run, particularly with the right outside foot on every turn, my toe was put through an incredible amount of abuse every day for thirteen years.

One doctor we visited prescribed custom orthotics,

molded to the contour of my feet, for support. Another ordered cortisone shots. And while those did help to mask the pain, over time the joint was destroyed. By 2007, I'd had four shots. Although it helped a bit, I knew I was headed down a path of no return. The cartilage that protected the joint would eventually wear completely down.

Starting in 2007, I taped my toe every single day. My physical trainer had developed a technique to support the toe that resembled a soft cast. In conjunction with caring for that toe with heat and continued cortisone injections, I was able to keep running through the pain.

I knew that one day I'd need to have surgery, but I planned to put it off as long as I could. I wanted to avoid missing the training time I'd lose during recovery as well as the unforeseen complications that were always possible.

But it was getting harder and harder to postpone that day.

Searching for Help

My husband Ross had introduced me to a doctor he knew from the NFL. He assured me that the surgery my toe needed was simple and straightforward. While I'm sure that could be true, especially in the hands of a talented surgeon, I'd also heard horror stories of athletes who experienced career-ending complications in the wake of "simple" surgeries.

As the 2012 Olympics approached, the doctor urged me to have the surgery with enough time to recuperate before the games. While I knew I needed it, something inside felt unsettled about agreeing to the surgery before the Games. I decided to wait.

In October, three months after winning gold in the 400, I checked in to New York City Hospital in the hopes that surgery would provide the relief I was after.

Relief, though, was not what I experienced.

If my pain prior to the surgery had been a 9 on a scale from 1 to 10, it shot up to a 15 after the procedure! If I had known how excruciating it would be, I might have chosen to limp along the way I'd been, managing the pain the best I could.

Post-surgery, I had no mobility in the joint. But I'd been told that in order to heal, I needed to keep moving the joint. I was assured that it would become more flexible and gain more mobility.

One day after practice, I complained to my dad, "Dad, something really isn't right. I feel like I'm breaking the bone."

Because he'd heard the same instructions I'd heard, he kept encouraging, "Keep trying, San. Keep trying."

Several months later I was desperate, and I turned to a doctor I'd seen before in Houston. Showing me the x-rays, he pointed to bits of bones. The shards of bone looked like remnants from a nail file.

He exclaimed, "I don't know how you ran on this for three months!"

I'd run on it for three months because not running wasn't an option. Like my dad suggested, I kept trying. After all, we'd been assured that doing so would loosen the joint. But, as my intuition and body had told me, I was only tearing up my toe further, breaking the bone as I ran.

In 2013, I was forced to undergo a second surgery. It repaired some of the damage, but I continued to suffer with daily pain.

In 2015, an airline passenger sharing my row exited by climbing over me. In the process, all of his body weight landed on my already-traumatized big right toe. As he apologized, I yelped in excruciating pain. Barely able to limp off the plane, I was in the operating room again within a few months.

For the last four years of my running career, I battled a silent, invisible foe. When the fiery blast of shooting pain would dart through my roots, I tried my best to stand strong.

I'm Not Alone. You're Not Alone.

Pain can be wildly isolating. As much as my family cared for me and wanted to relieve my suffering, I was the one who had to bear it. Through tears, and through clenched teeth, I could describe the pain to them, but I bore it alone.

When I stood on the podium, as I did in London in 2012, I knew that what people saw was my wide smile and Team USA uniform. I looked like I didn't have a care in the world. When I see those pictures, there isn't an ounce of pain in my smile, even though I remember feeling it that day.

The perception of perfection isn't a foreign feeling. We're exposed to it every day on social media! We see people's successes, but we're not privy to the entirety of their stories. So while they might look great on the outside, even people who seem to be living the dream face the same kind of obstacles and hurts you face. The win is in hurdling over the obstacles and pushing past the pain. The NBA finals are a great example. Those games are coming at the tail end of a season with over eighty games. Most of the athletes in the finals are pretty dinged up! Many are living with aches and pains, but they push through the entire season to be named as champions.

Pro athletes can't always wait until we're functioning at 100 percent to reach our goals. Neither can you! If you're waiting for the perfect moment to chase your dreams, you might be waiting forever. *Now is the moment.* Believe it can happen and prepare your heart and mind and body for success!

Everyone experiences obstacles they must overcome. One of mine has been my wily, difficult toe. Others, who might look awesome on the outside, are healing from emotional or physical abuse. Even that family at church that acts perfect and looks perfect is much more real and flawed than you'd imagine. Off Snapchat, various slim girls are battling eating disorders. After they've posted to Instagram, other ones fall into their beds, exhausted with depression. And the list goes on.

No one who saw one of my Nike ads knew I was battling a skin disease. They couldn't tell I was in pain each waking moment. They didn't know the private struggles I faced.

I suspect you have your own obstacles that not everyone can see. Maybe you struggle with a learning disorder. Maybe your home life is more difficult than even your friends know. Maybe you're caught in the grip of an addiction and you have no idea how you'll ever break free. Maybe you've made a choice you never dreamed you'd make.

Sister, I've been there, and I want you to hear that you are not alone. Social media might try and convince you that everyone else has it all together and you are the only one who struggles. The only one who stumbles. The only one who suffers. Trust me, it's not true.

If you find yourself in a lonely place today, access your resources. Confide in a parent. Talk to a friend. Pray. Seek wisdom in Scripture. Share with a trusted guide. Put yourself in communication with God and with others who can reflect what is most true: that you are loved and you are not alone.

Don't Quit

Overcoming obstacles and following through to reach your goals is going to look different in different situations. Sometimes it appears glamorous: you'll receive the award, get the scholarship, or score the winning goal. Other times, following through to meet your goals doesn't look like much of anything at all.

In 2008, about a year after my toe started giving me real trouble, I was the best women's 400 runner in the world. When I arrived at the Olympics in Beijing, I'd won every race in which I'd competed that year.

Before I got on the plane for China, though, I was in the midst of a spiritual and emotional crisis. The night before the race, my spirit was so uneasy and I felt so unworthy. As a result, I was unable to sleep.

Typically, when I show up on the track for a meet, I walk with a confident posture. I have a big smile on my face. I'm grateful to be there and ready to run. But when I stepped into lane 7 for the 400 finals, I was in a dark place, personally. When the announcer introduced me, and the camera showed my face to the stadium and the world, Shari knew something wasn't right. She told me later that she'd thought to herself, "That's not my sister."

If I ever wanted to be in the right head space, the 400 meter Olympic finals was when I wanted to be on top of my game. But because of the personal burden I was carrying in my heart, I couldn't will myself to be there.

At the start of the race, I got off the way I'd wanted to. Coming off the turn, I had a strong lead.

Those moments are still so vivid in my memory. In each Olympics, the signature Olympic rings are typically painted across the track, midway down the straightaway. It's beautiful. But as I passed them, I felt a cramp in my hamstring. Unwilling to obey my mind, my body started to falter. It's hard to watch those tapes. In the last twenty meters, two runners passed me to dip across the finish line to claim first and second place. I was disappointed to win the bronze, and my face showed it.

I was the third-fastest 400 sprinter in the world, what many would consider an impressive accomplishment, but I'd never felt more awful.

Dragging the back of my hand across my face, I wiped tears from my cheeks. I had about forty-five minutes before medals were awarded, and my mother found her way to me and comforted me. As I changed into my Team USA warm-ups for the ceremony, though, I was still fighting back sobs. Taking deep breaths, trying to think of anything besides my defeat, I vowed to hold myself together.

For a moment, I did.

One of the Chinese officials, a man about fifty years old, was in charge of leading the three medalists from a staging area to the pubic podium.

On the way, he playfully teased, "What happened? We have your name on the gold medal!"

His words threw open the brittle makeshift door holding my powerful emotions at bay. Without warning, I began sobbing again.

All these years I've remembered that Chinese official because his surprise represented a world of track enthusiasts who were certain I'd win the gold that year. I wasn't the only one struggling to make sense of the defeat. Those who followed the sport were flabbergasted by the loss. Because I'd been suffering emotionally, because I'd been feeling so unworthy, I had a hunch that, unconsciously, I'd unwittingly participated in sabotaging my own race.

Redemption

After that race, I had no interest in staying in the Olympic village with the other athletes. I just wanted to nurse my wounds, surrounded by family, in a quieter space. I took a bus designated for athletes to the village to grab some of my things, and then I took a public bus to a house my family had rented. Though I thought I knew which bus to take, nothing looked familiar. Desperate, helpless, I began bawling again.

When I reflected on that disorienting experience later, it felt as though the turmoil I'd carried in my heart had been made manifest: I was lost. But when I felt most overwhelmed, with no idea how to get to the people who represented "home," I felt God wrapping his arms around me, assuring me, "You'll be fine. You're loved."

They were the holy words I most wanted and needed to hear.

As if heaven-sent, an American fan recognized me despite my smeared makeup, and asked, "You know where you're going?"

Admitting I didn't, I described the neighborhood where my family was staying. I'd been there several times and remembered some landmarks. Thankfully, he was able to point me to the right bus line and I made it to my parents' place.

When I was out of tears, it was time to return to the stadium for the 4x4 relay. At that time, American women dominated the relay. In fact, we'd been so dominant in past seasons that our anchor runner usually received the stick with such a lead that the last lap was more like a victory lap than a competition lap!

But, in the finals, my teammate was passed on the third leg. That meant the Russian team had completed their hand-off before I touched our stick.

Remember how bummed I'd been about my defeat in the 400? Well, my sadness had been replaced by a fury of resolve. There was no way, I'd determined, that I was going to leave Beijing without a gold. I ran the race of my life—for myself, for my teammates, for my country—and slipped into the lead within five meters of the finish line. We won!

That was another holy moment on the track for me. Although I remain firm in my conviction that God's not counting up wins and losses, I'm equally sure that God does make both *meaningful* when we offer them to him. And that win was soaked with meaning for me. In fact, I saw it as a beautiful picture of God's love.

Grace

You may have a weight you've been carrying that's slowed you down from reaching your goals. Maybe you've been sidelined by injury, like I was. Or maybe you've been carrying a weight of shame and guilt. Or maybe you're haunted by past failures. Believe me, I've been there too. But nothing you've suffered, and nothing you've done, disqualifies you from reaching your goals.

I encourage you to pay attention to that little voice that condemns you. That hisses in your ear that the obstacles you've faced, or the choices you've made, disqualify you from the good God has for you. Nothing could be farther from the truth. God is a gracious God, and has created you for good things. The voice that accuses is not God's voice.

When you hear, "What happened? We have your name on the gold medal!", listen again for God's still, small voice assuring you, "See, I have engraved you on the palms of my hands" (Isaiah 49:16).

RIGHT ON TRACK CHALLENGE

Have the obstacles in your life slowed you down?

- What is the biggest obstacle you've faced?
- How have you dealt with it?
- In what ways is it keeping you from reaching your goal today?
- What do you need to do to keep pressing on?

Notice the hurdle that's been a stumbling block for you. Then write down one action step you can take today to move closer to reaching your goals.

CHAPTER 14

IT TAKES A VILLAGE

No matter what your dream is, you need supporters by your side.

I feel like the luckiest girl because the members of my family have been my most loyal supporters. Before I ever graced the pages of *Sports Illustrated* or was featured on ESPN, Dad, Mom, and Shari were my first entourage. In every race, I felt strengthened by the strong presence of my family. Walking into track meets with the three of them around me, I felt invincible.

When we arrived in the United States when I was eleven, my mom and dad created an amazing gym for me to use at home. Our two-car garage was filled with a weight bench, free weights, a pull-up machine, medicine balls, physical therapy balls, yoga mats, and jump ropes. My dad even installed a mirror on the wall so we could ensure I was using the best form. I know that there are elite athletes in developing countries without access to the abundant resources I had at my fingertips.

Mom

My mom was my first fitness trainer. Though most people who've followed my career—from my childhood in Jamaica through my final Olympic trial—have seen what a huge part of my success my dad was, fewer know about my mom.

She. Is. Incredible.

She ran a clothing store and a gym in Jamaica, and she helped me develop my skills in the weight room. She taught me how to do squats and how to bench press. Though I'd eventually work with some of the world's best trainers, she was the first person to push me in the weight room.

When I released my agent in 2006, my mom was working for American Express.

I called her one afternoon and asked her to be my agent.

"If you and Dad worked with me," I begged, "I'd be better off."

Because they were familiar with how I felt about my first agent, she knew it was true.

Two weeks later, she quit her job and came to work for me. It was such a great fit. If you know what agents do for athletes, then you know they're supposed to be like mama bears anyway! They make sure the cub eats. They protect them from predators. And the very best ones don't let any harm come to their cubs. I know that not every parent should manage their child's athletic career, but it was a great move for my mom and me. She was the smart, wise, mama bear protector I needed.

During the ten years she was my agent, she negotiated all of my contracts for competitions. She traveled to all my meets. She made sure my coach and other support staff were paid. She booked all my travel for competitions. Basically, she took care of hundreds of details no one ever sees so that I could be who we both believed I was born to be.

She was, and still is, a precious gift in my life.

Dad

Like my mom, the impact of my dad's investment of time, money, and energy into me and my career is immeasurable. Very few people can understand the level of commitment he has demonstrated over the first three decades of my life.

In my earliest years, before college and my pro career, when races were typically filmed or televised, my dad knew that recording and reviewing my races would be critical for my development as an athlete. That meant that, no matter what seat number was printed on his ticket, he'd be perched right above the finish line. If any dutiful security guard tried to thwart him, he'd communicate, with his body, his face, his voice, "I shall not be moved."

When I became a professional athlete and began to train with Coach Hart, I was still taking classes at the University of Texas in Austin. But Coach was ninety minutes away at Baylor in Waco. Though my folks were still living in Florida at the time, my dad moved to Austin to drive me to and from practice! My mom was able to move and join him the next year, but he spent a whole season taking care of me. Though I knew how to drive, he was afraid I'd be too tired and didn't want me on the road three hours a day.

Dad never minded being my chauffeur and chef. He cooked the foods my body needed to be in peak shape, and he juiced fruits and vegetables for me to drink every day. He even ended up being my sports psychologist! Yes, he examined my body mechanics and helped me analyze my physical performance in races, but he also understood, and helped me understand, my mental game.

If my mom ended up getting to do the cool stuff—traveling with me to races in Europe and photo shoots at Nike headquarters—my dad chose to take on the unglamorous jobs. He'd run across the track after a hard effort to bring me a bottle of water in the brutal Texas heat. He'd record my workout routines and times in a journal for me. But Dad never complained, and never seemed to mind that Mom was having all the fun. He just supported me each day in his quiet, steady way.

Since my first practice as a little girl in Jamaica, he's always been in the trenches with me.

Shari

I've mentioned that Shari was a unique sister. She has been one of the best gifts in my life.

When we first moved to Florida, two Jamaican girls figuring out how to be Americans, we shared a bedroom. Late at night, I'd share my dreams with her about running and college and boys and the Olympics.

Sometimes, when one child in the family garners extra attention from parents and others—perhaps because they have a special talent, like I did, or maybe because they have a special challenge, like a child with an intellectual or physical disability—the siblings suffer. Consciously or unconsciously, they feel they don't receive the attention they want and need. I suppose it's a tribute to my parents that Shari didn't suffer like that. But it's also a tribute to who Shari is.

Shari instilled a lot of confidence in me, and you can't do that if you're not someone who already has confidence in themselves. She did, and she still does. She had a good head on her shoulders, knew who she was, and never wanted to be anyone other than herself.

As I listen for her voice in my ear today, I hear her hollering from the stands, "Let's go, Sanya! You can do it! Nobody can beat you!" When I watch recordings of my professional races, I swear I can hear Shari screaming in the stands. In many ways, she was my sure footing. As I'd crouch in the blocks, still and quiet while the stadium held its collective breath, I could feel her confidence in me.

When my mom and dad had to worry about body mechanics and contracts and juices and airline delays, Shari was free to simply be my number one fan. And I couldn't ask for a better one. She has come to every meet she could. Even when I was in my first year of college in Texas, while my family was still in Florida, she and my parents would fly out to support me in competitions.

Honestly, she had to put up with what a lot of siblings wouldn't choose, because most places she went she was known as "Sanya's sister." Yet she was never jealous. She never complained. She was always supportive.

My husband Ross and I have gotten used to being "recognized" out in public. Depending on whether someone is a track fan or football fan, we're used to hearing, "Are you Sanya's husband?" or "Are you Aaron's wife?" We smile and proudly admit that we are.

A few years ago, I had the coolest experience when Ross and I were out at the mall in Austin, where my parents and Shari now also live.

We were walking past the food court when a young woman approached me and asked, "Are you Shari's sister? You look just like her! She does my hair!" I couldn't have been prouder, beaming as I responded, "I am!"

If you know how hard it is to find someone truly gifted with hair, you know that young lady probably felt like she was meeting the sister of a superstar!

That moment, as I swelled with pride to be Shari Richards' sister, I felt like I was standing on the podium.

Coach Hart

When I started working with Coach Hart in 2005, he'd not yet coached a female athlete who'd seen the kinds of success his male athletes like Michael Johnson and Jeremy Warner had. But he took a chance on a University of Texas girl, and I've been grateful ever since that he did.

Coach Hart was in his early seventies when he took me on. One of the things I loved most about him was that he was solid. He wasn't easily shaken. He was the rock of confidence and experience that I needed. He was also a strong Christian, with the confidence that God has a plan.

When I planned my wedding for my twenty-fifth

birthday, I hadn't calculated that it coincided with a huge Big 12 conference track meet. Coach Hart had attended that meet religiously for over fifty years.

When he received the invitation to my wedding, he was bummed.

"Oh, San, is there any way you can change it?" he begged.

While I shared his passion for the sport, I was *not* going to change the date of my wedding.

The day Ross received me as his bride, Coach Hart was there to celebrate with us. That's the kind of man he was. Other coaches in the conference couldn't believe that he'd missed the meet. I felt so loved by that generous gesture. Coach has two sons, but no daughters. He'd already given me so much—traveling with me, being away from his family during the collegiate season—and he showed up for the most important day of my life.

Coach Hart wasn't one to display a lot of emotion. Some might even describe him as "ice cold." But I'd like to think I melted his heart. I even got him to start hugging! A coach who worked with him for thirty years remarked to me, "You changed him! He's a soft teddy bear now!"

Your Crew

I could not have experienced the success I've enjoyed without this amazing crew. Each one has made countless sacrifices to make what I've done possible. I could never have reached the finish line, could never have stepped up to the podium, without the day-in and day-out support they've provided.

I know that sounds like a cliché, something you'd hear from someone in a ball gown receiving an Oscar, but it's true! My people are amazing.

I've been telling you about the amazing people who have been the biggest cheerleaders in my life, and it's my hope and prayer that you have this kind of support in your own life.

Maybe, like me, you have a whole fleet of supporters. Maybe, when you close your eyes, you can visualize a huge crew of your own fans—wearing T-shirts that say "Team Ebony" or "Team Zoe" or "Team Emma"—who always have your back and always show up for you.

But I realize that's not always the case.

I encourage you to look for the kind eyes, the open ears, the loving voice of just *one person* who's been part of your cheerleading team. Maybe you have a grandmother who thinks you are amazing. Her eyes reflect God's eyes. Or maybe a friend's mom noticed you and spent time listening to you. Her ears represent God's ears. Or maybe a volunteer with your church youth group has given advice that helped you as you thought about your future. That voice echoes with the wisdom of God's own voice.

A proverb attributed to African culture says, "It takes a village to raise a child." It means that a child will be best nurtured when the entire community contributes to her upbringing. I would say that God uses the village to bless the child. That was certainly true in my life, in the ways I was cared for by my family, my coach, and others. I hope you can recognize who those faithful "villagers" have been in your life. If you can't see them yet, ask God to show you their faces and reveal their names.

You are worth loving. You are worth protecting. You are worth respecting. And because you've been made to reach for your dreams, God provides cheerleaders and supporters to help you achieve your goals.

Who Are You Cheering For?

Encouragement is never a one-way street. Yes, God has allowed me to be surrounded with precious ones who've stood with me and for me, but God has also called me to cheer others on to victory as well.

Since my husband Ross and I met, I've been his biggest fan. In college, I'd attend his football games, proudly wearing my big "My Boyfriend's #31" button! My heart's desire has always been to see him be great. In fact, over the years, we've pushed each other to be the best we can be. I have loved being his cheerleader and seeing him enjoy success as an athlete.

I also support my friends in the track world. When my friend Bershawn Jackson runs, I'm usually more nervous than he is! Despite my own bumps and bruises at the 2008 Olympics in Beijing, it was a joy to see him stand on the podium for his performance in the 400 hurdles. I've been rooting for some of my friends—like Nichole Denby and Lauryn Williams—since we were in college! The three of us formed a bond in 2002 when we competed in the World Juniors meet. I've cheered for them, followed their careers, and wished them every success. It's been as much fun supporting them as it has been supporting Ross.

Of course being a faithful cheerleader doesn't just happen on the track and the gridiron. We all need cheerleaders! I have found such joy in partnering with Shari as she's started her own company and hair salon. Her support helped me be great, and I hope mine has buoyed her as well. I continue to be amazed at her talent, drive, and business savvy. My hope is that I'm able to reflect for her—with my face and voice and body—all the beauty and gifts God has given her.

If you're an athlete, you might have friends who've shown up to support you, waving a sign or screaming their lungs out. If you're competitive academically, you may have a classmate who studies with you and pushes you to be your best. If you're an artist and post your work on Facebook, your cheerleaders are the ones who share your stuff and brag about your work. If you're a singer or a musician, they come to your concerts. If you write, it might be the aunt or teacher or friend who's taken the time to read your work and offer you feedback. As you look around, I hope you'll start to see the beautiful village of supporters who reflect God's own delight and support for you.

No matter what your dream is, you need fans by your side.

RIGHT ON TRACK CHALLENGE

Are you able to recognize those who've been cheerleaders in your life?

- In your earliest years, who was someone who cheered for you?
- Today, who do you turn to when you need to be seen, known, and loved?
- Who is someone that *you* show up for consistently, helping them to reach their goals?
- Who might you begin cheering for?

Think of one person who has been with you and for you on your own journey to reach your goals. Take fifteen minutes to write them a letter—a real one, on paper, in an envelope, with a stamp—thanking them for being your cheerleader.

CHAPTER 15

SAVOR THE WIN

The year I got married, I experienced my first season-ending injury.

The grand calendar of the track and field world has a predictable annual rhythm: World Championships, Olympics, World Championships, year off. Then the cycle begins again.

In 2009, one of the World Championship years, I ran my best season to date. The pinnacle of that great season was that I'd won the 400 at the Worlds. I was flying high. As I was planning my wedding, I knew I was heading into a year without one of those major competitions.

Though the wedding in February of 2010 was perfect, the season was not. Early in the season I tore my quad. You may be saying to yourself, "Not the worst season for an injury. No major competition." And you'd be right. My team and I decided that the best thing to do would be to take the season off to recover. We'd rehab and I'd be back. It definitely felt like the right move.

In the 2011 season, though, I really wasn't running like Sanya Richards-Ross. I had recovered from the physical injury, but I wasn't able to compete at my best mentally. A tear in the quad muscle is very painful, so even after the physical therapist cleared me to run, I was still hesitant. I just wasn't able to get going in 2011 and run my best race.

If you've ever had a painful injury, you might be able to relate. When you're hurting, your body compensates by walking gingerly, bending carefully, or reaching gently. An instinct kicks in to avoid pain. But once your injury heals, you might still move in some of those same ways—to avoid pain.

I really struggled that season. In fact, I lost more races than I won, which was very unusual. Especially after the beautiful season I'd had in 2009. During the 2011 season, I only had one good race. It was a meet in London during our regular season competition. Coach Hart was there, my mom was there, and my physical therapist was there. The whole team saw me run like the old Sanya. I broke 50, running the 400 in 49.6 seconds, the fastest time in the world. As I was running and crossing the finish line, I caught a glimmer of my old self.

Oh, yeah, this is what it feels like: push, pace, position, poise.

Oh, yeah, this is what it feels like to fly.

Running an excellent race makes all the grueling training worth it. The endless rigor of every early-morning practice, every sit-up, every protein shake, every mile logged fades into the background as my legs stretch out in front of me, doing what they've been trained to do.

I was back. And as I looked forward toward the 2012 London Olympics, it was time to believe in myself again.

When I'd competed in the Athens Olympics in 2004, I

was nineteen. I was thrilled to have made it to the Games. But 2008 had been different. When I'd gone to the Games in Beijing, I'd been struggling emotionally and spiritually. It had been a terribly difficult experience and I fought to even hold it together as I received my bronze medal. I wish I could say that experience was completely behind me and never entered my mind. Unfortunately, that's not true. With London on the horizon in 2012, I trained hard during 2011 and 2012. I kept my eyes fixed on the win. But if I turned my head to the side for a moment, I saw Beijing in the rearview mirror. And I was determined to do better.

I started 2012 training like a mad woman. That's the part you never see when an athlete stands atop the podium to receive a medal. You don't see the grueling physical and mental work that goes into being a champion. I was completely dedicated and I trained hard. I ran longer miles. I did two thousand sit-ups every day. I drank plenty of water. I ate well, juicing veggies and fruits. If you've ever seen the movie *Rocky*—or at least the classic scene where he runs up the seventy-two steps of the Philadelphia Art Museum during his intense training—you can kind of imagine what my life was like. Eyes on the prize, I was single minded.

I don't always run the indoor winter track season, but that year I did. In fact, I won my first World indoor title in Istanbul.

But then I went to Jamaica and lost to Jamaican sprinter Novlene Williams. Losing is bad enough, but when the biggest track fans in the world go wild for the woman who beat you, it's pretty brutal. The land that was so good to me as a child proved harder to conquer as an adult! I knew I'd been prepared to run well physically, but I hadn't been able to run the race I wanted to run.

The loss was a very emotional one. Later that night, I was talking to Ross and my dad on the balcony of our hotel room about the race. The second hundred meters of the race is where I'm supposed to pace, but I was so pumped up and anxious that I went too fast. That meant that in the final one hundred meters, I was too tired to take the win. That said, I wasn't beat by twenty meters. Or ten meters. I lost by a "lean"—just a tenth of a second. While no loss is easy, that's a really hard way to go!

As we were dissecting the race, the way we always do, I had a mini meltdown. I felt disappointed, sad, and confused.

My dad, who I'm sure was also disappointed, put the loss in perspective for me. "Forget it. Move on. Don't make a mountain out of a molehill."

I wanted to protest, but in my heart I knew he was right.

After Jamaica, I ran the Prefontaine. That was the year I had that amazing moment with the Lord on the track when the wind and my heart were still and at peace. And . . . I won!

I was ready for the Olympics.

London

I went to London filled with confidence. With the exception of that difficult race in Jamaica, I'd been winning all my individual races that year. I felt physically and mentally strong. But of course, the biggest challenge for me in London was going to be releasing the enduring memory of that huge disappointment and staying focused on what was before me.

London included some off-the-track drama for a lot of the athletes, including me. International Olympic Committee Rule 40 says that—with the exception of official IOC sponsors—no competitor, coach, trainer, or official who participates in the Olympic Games can allow his or her name, picture, or sports performances to be used for advertising. Specifically, there's a blackout window that begins nine days before opening ceremonies until three days after the closing ceremonies.

Honestly, though, I was going to be okay. Nike, and my other sponsors, took care of me. I was concerned for a lot of the other athletes who were working with smaller sponsors. Disallowing Olympians from giving shout-outs to their smaller sponsors—a local car dealership or a regional sporting goods chain—when they were most visible was a deterrent for businesses to sponsor these talented and deserving athletes.

When all the athletes had arrived in London, but before the start of the Games, I booked a large room for an hour to discuss the issue together. About one hundred athletes showed up. Nick Symmonds, also a track and field athlete, was fired up like I was and had also been speaking out.

I challenged the room, "I know that not everyone is paid to be here. And for a lot of you it's limiting the money you can make. It's not fair. But we can take a stand together." I suggested that we use the hashtag #wedemandchange, the slogan Adam Nelson (an Olympic gold medalist) and I came up with the night before, and all of the athletes who agreed tweeted it out. The hashtag went viral, elevating the conversation within the sporting world. Because our meeting was the night before our team's big press conference, and because I was one of the more well-known athletes to do it, I was bombarded by the media.

Some fans gave me grief, calling me ungrateful. But there were also plenty of others who called out what they saw as the IOC's greed. These critics claimed that the IOC was more concerned about catering to its sponsors than caring for its athletes.

I mention this hubbub because, in the days leading up to my big races, I was being viewed by the world not only as an athlete who'd faltered in 2008 but now also as a big-mouth activist.

My teammate Khadevis Robinson, a middle-distance runner, was concerned about me the way a big brother would be.

One day during warm-ups he gently said, "What you're doing is really admirable. But I don't want this to take away from you winning the gold."

I felt the love in his concern.

"I feel like God's on my side," I assured him. "I'm doing the right thing, and whatever happens, I'm okay with it. I'm proud that I'm speaking out for athletes."

I came by my conviction honestly. My dad was a lot like

me—a rebel. He'd always been passionate about doing what was right and supported me 100 percent. My mom, though, shared some of the same concerns Khadevis did. She agreed with what I was about, but didn't like the extra attention it brought. Her advice was to fly under the radar so I could focus on winning my race. I understood that she just wanted to protect me. Ultimately, I chose to speak because I felt compelled to honor the convictions God had laid on my conscience.

While the fervor of #wedemandchange was still simmering in the media, I shifted my attention to the job I'd come to London to do. Focusing on my race, I set my mind on victory.

The Big Race

The individual 400 in the 2012 race was, arguably, the most important race of my career. As it had been in 2008, Olympic gold was at stake.

Typically, I breezed through the prelims. I wasn't matched with my fiercest rivals, so those early races had begun to feel like "checking the box." When I was on the warm-up track, getting ready for the first prelim, it began raining. The first several heats of runners had to run in the rain. But the moment I stepped out on the track, the sun came out. Seriously, it was like a movie. I received that as a sign that God was smiling on me and this was going to be *my* Olympics.

I did breeze through the prelims, but the final was very intense.

Running in the Olympics is a different beast than other

races. After we warm up, we're called in to a staging area where we wait for up to an hour. We're corralled with our competitors three times longer than we are in any other meet. If you've watched any of that backstage footage during the Olympic games, you'll see some athletes zoned out listening to music with headphones. Others might be stretching. Some might be praying. Others will be shaking out their muscles. The mind games that happen from sharing that same prep space are intense! And it's often hardest on young athletes. Because of the meticulous schedule being kept, we're moved down a hallway, from room to room, getting closer to the track. It adds to the gravity of the race we're facing, which is already pretty fierce.

When we were finally released onto the track, I was in lane 6, and Novlene Williams, who'd beat me in Jamaica, was in lane 7.

Even the hoopla on the track takes longer. The introductions are grander and the audience's reactions, cheering among fans from the various countries represented, takes longer too. As the announcer was heralding the Russian runner in lane 5, I had a flashback to how that moment had felt for me four years earlier. That's when Shari had looked up at the big screen and thought to herself, "That's not my sister." I had been undone emotionally, and it had showed. That's why, when the announcer spoke my name in London, I had my game face on. I gave a big smile as I waved, to say, "I'm ready!"

I was.

I was prepared for all the predictable distractions: windy

weather, rainy weather, trash talk, races running behind schedule. My head was in the right place and I was ready to do battle.

But when the announcer got to lane 8, the response from the crowd was unnerving. Christine Ohuruogu, running for Great Britain, was defending her Olympic gold title from 2008. The odds of running in the Olympics on your home turf as a defending champion are miniscule. And her family lived just one mile from the stadium! If ever a crowd was dishing out hometown love, this was it. When the announcer spoke her name, the fans went wild for Ohuruogu.

There were three minutes between that crazy cheering and the start of the race. Three minutes for me to get my head back in a good space. Three minutes to focus on my race and breathe a prayer to God. As I stepped into the blocks, I spoke in my mind, "I can do all this through him who gives me strength." (Philippians 4:13)

BANG!

At the crack of the gunshot, I got out of the blocks hard. Russian Antonina Krivoshapka, in lane 5, also got out really, really fast! Because the Russians don't compete a lot on the track circuit, I hadn't raced against her often and wasn't used to running beside someone with that much power at the front end of the race. Typically, I'm the fastest person in the first two hundred meters. Because my head was in the race, I reminded myself, "Relax. Pace . . . pace . . . pace . . ." I was determined to run *my* race.

She was leading on the inside, but as we got to the turn we

both picked up speed. Coming off the turn, though, DeeDee Trotter was in the lead. Usually DeeDee didn't turn on the power until the last fifty, so when I saw her in front I thought, *Sanya, you've got to get going.*

I got going, but continued to run the race that Coach and I had planned.

In the final fifty meters, Christine Ohuruogu turned it up and came down the final stretch strong. The crowd was frantic. Knowing the increasing roar of the crowd meant someone was right on my heels, I dipped forward for a huge lean over the finish line.

Running my race, I made it to the finish line first!

Though the race had been close, with Christine Ohuruogu sliding past the finish line a fraction of a second after me, I was confident I'd won. I kept my eyes on the board, but the names weren't being posted. Though I'd felt my body fly over the line first, these kinds of delays were always nerve-racking. Had I committed a violation? What was the holdup?

I mentally willed the officials to post my name, "Please be me . . . please be me . . ."

I won't lie. There was a moment of doubt.

Because of the noise . . .

Because of the delay . . .

Because of Beijing . . .

When I'd started the race, Shari had shouted out to me during my warm-up lap on the big track. So I'd been able to spot Shari, Ross, and my amazing cousin Yollie at the twenty-meter mark. I looked over and saw them pumping their fists.

If they had any of the glimmers of doubt I had, they weren't showing it.

In the most magical display I'd ever seen, the results were finally posted.

1st Place: United States. Sanya Richards-Ross. 49.55.
2nd Place: Great Britain. Christine Ohuruogu. 49.70.
3rd Place: United States. DeeDee Trotter. 49.72.
4th Place: Botswana. Amantle Montsho. 49.75

The delay hadn't been about first place at all! The officials wanted to be certain that the excruciatingly thin differences between second, third, and fourth place were accurate.

About thirty of my friends and family members had traveled to London to support me. In an amazing feat, considering how tight security was, everyone I knew made it down to the front row in the wake of my victory. As I ran my victory lap, I reached over to give them all hugs. Unlike the race I'd just run where *nothing* could have stopped me, I stopped about a hundred times!

My favorite stop was at my husband. Because of his own rigorous schedule, Ross had never been able to make it to the Olympics before. For the first time, I was able to run over and kiss him! Even today I cherish the picture of that moment I got to share with him.

Take a Lap

It's important to take a victory lap.

When you've worked hard for something, whether it's

building an award-winning robot, getting into the college of your dreams, completing your first marathon, or taking gold in a speech competition, it's okay to relish the victory. In fact, it's important to do it.

Too often, we move too fast. We finish a volleyball season and start basketball training the next day. We rock the ACT, and the moment it's over we're looking up dates to take the SAT. We finish high school and start registering for college courses. Those of us who are motivated to reach our dreams can often be in a constant state of moving forward to the next thing.

I confess, I've been guilty.

Dating? I'd love to be engaged. Engaged? I'm ready to be married. Married? Ready to get back to competition. Competition? Twenty-nine months until the next Olympics! Retirement from running? I'm ready to be a mom.

There's nothing wrong with having goals, but once we reach them, they're worth celebrating! They're worth savoring. They're worth cherishing.

Olympic tradition requires a victory lap from the winner. But, honestly, if they didn't require it, we wouldn't do it. And we'd probably think those who *did* do it were a little conceited. But there's something about it that's so *right*. The race was over in fifty seconds, but that victory lap took me fifteen minutes! It was worth taking fifteen minutes to celebrate the fulfillment of that lifetime dream.

It's worth celebrating your wins too. Did you build a bedframe with your own two hands? Take a lap around your house! Did you work your tail off to finally earn a B in a math class? Take a lap around the school! Raise enough money babysitting over the year to go on a mission trip with your youth group? Run around your block! If it's not running, figure out what your victory lap looks like. Maybe it means making a special dinner for your family. Or eating out at a restaurant. Maybe you and a sibling take a special road trip. I encourage you to celebrate your victories.

And as you do, always give thanks to the Giver of all good gifts (James 1:17).

RIGHT ON TRACK CHALLENGE

When you've reached a goal, it's tempting to move on to the next one. But I encourage you to pause and celebrate your successes as an expression of gratitude.

- Have you made a practice of celebrating your successes?
- How have you celebrated in the past? Dinner with family? Movie with friends?
- Is there a milestone—a recital, a competition, an exhibit— that you can celebrate during this season of your life?
- How do you invite God into your celebration?

Don't miss out on savoring the sweetness of victory now because you're gunning for the next win. What is one accomplishment you can celebrate today?

CHAPTER 16

ONWARD AND UPWARD

Though I'd announced that I'd be retiring after the 2016 Olympic Games in Rio, my end came a bit sooner than I would have chosen.

Before the Olympic trials at the end of June, I'd already been suffering with toe pain for three years. That daily affliction started to drain the love of running from my heart. I never believed I could say those words, but every day had begun to feel like a battle with my toe. To protect that broken-down digit, I'd unintentionally begun running on the outside of my foot. That, of course, caused other issues. I showed up for the trials in Eugene because I thought it was the right thing to do. But even in advance of that meet, I'd been weighing when was the true time to stop. A lot went into that decision.

I'd accomplished most of my dreams and goals. I didn't want to do further damage to my toe that would lead to a life in which I wasn't able to walk. Ross and I were ready to think about expanding our family.

The trick was to balance each one of those thoughts with the factors that were pulling me to compete in Rio: my love of running and the drive to always be reaching for the next goal. I'd nurtured that drive for three decades, and it wasn't easy to just turn it off!

Just a few weeks before traveling to Eugene for the Olympic trials, I pulled my hamstring. In the days leading right up to the trials I hadn't run much, let alone sprinted. I wanted to give my body every opportunity to heal.

My leg was taped for support, causing spectators and commentators to wonder how I'd perform. Before racing, I followed the timeline for our warm-up routine that Coach Hart had set up. Each drill was scripted to the minute. When I struggled to get through my 30–60–90 progressions, we both recognized that I had the power to burst, but lacked the strength to shift. It wasn't clear to either of us if my leg could hold up in a race around the track.

With gentleness in his voice, Coach Hart offered, "Sanya, you don't have to do this."

It was like he was giving me permission to be less than superhuman. I felt loved by the kindness.

"Coach," I countered, "I didn't come all this way not to try."

As I stepped toward the blocks, I couldn't anticipate what was about to happen. I knew my hamstring hadn't had the six weeks of recovery it required. I knew I might humiliate myself out there. But after years of keeping my head up, looking forward, and chasing excellence, I struggled to ignore that drive in the face of adversity.

At the sound of the starting gun, I took off with the pack. But I immediately knew that something was off.

Commentators narrating the race recognized, from the first step, that I'd been tentative out of the blocks. In the first fifty meters, I knew I wouldn't be able to finish the race. I tried to hold my position but was slowly losing ground. At the second turn, I had to pull up. As my legs slowed, there was no question in anyone's mind that my race was ending.

My *career* was ending.

Brimming with disappointment, I continued to jog around the track. After the other athletes had crossed the finish line, I continued around the track raising my arms and waving my thanks to the amazing crowd at Hayward Field.

Echoing my earliest races in Jamaica, a woman yelled, "We love you, Sanya!"

She wasn't alone. Many in the crowd rose to their feet, clapping and cheering for me. The lap that should have been painfully disappointing was instead bittersweet. I was sad my career was ending before the 2016 Olympics, but I also felt a flood of gratitude for the amazing support my fans had offered me over the years.

Before I was even able to catch my breath, a reporter was engaging me with questions.

"Man, this is tough for me," I shared honestly, chest still heaving for oxygen. "You know, when the season started I saw myself potentially defending my title, and just obstacle after obstacle. I thank God that I was able to come out here today, but when I tried to hit my next gear, my hamstring just locked up on me. I'm grateful for an amazing career and amazing fan support, and I'm excited for the next chapter of my life."

I went on to say, "I do want to go into broadcasting. That's one of the things I'm passionate about. I'm working on a book, wanting to inspire other people to be their best. And then, a mom. I want to start a family. So I'm excited about that."

Though one dream had ended, the seeds of the next had already been planted in my heart.

What Was Next

That final race had been on Saturday, July 2. It was a clear and sudden end to the career I'd been building for more than two decades. What I didn't know during that emotional finish was that the next chapter of my journey was going to start a lot sooner than I'd expected.

The following day, NBC called one of my managers, Lis Moss, to invite me to work with them as a commentator. Lis then called my mom, who was with me in Oregon. Both of them knew how crushed I was to release the dream of defending my title in my fourth Olympics. My mom assured Lis that she'd speak with me about it when the time was right.

After going out to dinner as a family, I was talking to Ross outside under some beautiful oak trees. Eugene was gorgeous in the summer.

Stepping outside of the home we'd rented, my mom gently asked if she could speak with me.

When she told me about the opportunity, I was blown

away. The door to Rio had barely closed, and God had already opened a new door. Feelings of disappointment and joy and sadness and gratitude collided in my heart, and I began to cry. The opportunity felt like such a gift. Because it's in my nature to always be strategizing my next move, it felt like a kindness from the Lord to be handed that good gift on a gold platter. I didn't have to chase it down. In that amazing opportunity, I heard God saying, "I got you, San. I got you."

I told my mom, "Let me talk to Ross. Give me a day and we'll get back to them."

As I expected, Ross was incredibly supportive. We called NBC on Monday morning and were having brunch with them the same day. They said they'd been watching me and felt like I had all the attributes they were looking for. They hadn't had a woman in the booth for over ten years, and had been looking for the right one.

Although it sounds crazy to say now, I was in the booth at Hayward Field by Wednesday! I got to commentate for the last three days of the trials, and it was amazing. Track has been the greatest blessing in my life, and I'll always love it. With this opportunity, I'd be able to contribute to the sport in a new way that really excited me.

For just a few short days, I thought I wasn't going to Rio. I was wrong.

Heading to Brazil

When NBC asked me that week to work as a commentator in Rio, I was thrilled.

That said, the decision of whether or not I would go wasn't one Ross and I took lightly. The outbreak of the Zika virus, which caused brain abnormalities in fetuses, had scared a lot of fans away from Rio. The virus was being transmitted through infected mosquitoes. Ross and I were eager to start a family. Did we want to risk it? A doctor working with NBC assured me that, because it was "winter" in Rio, there wouldn't be many mosquitoes. Her expertise and insights were helpful. Ross would have loved to have traveled with me, but because the virus lives longer in the bloodstreams of men than in women, we chose against doubling our chances and eventually decided I'd travel alone.

I have to tell you that any fans and athletes who chose not to go to Rio missed out. It was a beautiful country with amazing people. And I didn't see one mosquito my entire visit!

Just before the Games, the producer I expected to work with was injured and wasn't able to make the trip to Rio. The producer who took over the assignment for him had quite the sense of humor.

Seconds before I went live on air, he said, "Thirty seconds to thirty million! Be great!"

No pressure.

I was so nervous, and the reminder that thirty million people would be listening didn't help! I just kept reminding myself that talking on air about the athletes wasn't any different than dishing with my parents in our living room. And I'd been couch-commentating for years.

Thankfully, I held up under the pressure, getting more

and more comfortable every day. My parents could hear it too when they listened to the broadcasts. It was an incredibly fun experience with a great group of people, and I enjoyed the challenge of improving.

Working in Rio was a different beast than broadcasting in Eugene had been. At the trials, I already knew most of the American athletes. But in Rio, I had to study each night, reading up on the athletes and learning how to pronounce some pretty unique names!

Watching

A lot of people have asked me what it was like to be in Rio but not be running. I can honestly say that it was exciting to watch every race.

Except one.

The women's 400 meter was tough to watch.

Over the years I'd been running it, I'd fallen in love with the race. The strategy. Even the pain. My mind began to play tricks on me. Could I have continued to compete? If I'd given the injury time to heal, would I have come back in a few races? Why couldn't I have been healthy? But in the end, I knew that I'd done everything possible to make it work. I also believed that God had already been so good to me, and I wanted to live with gratitude for that instead of with regrets and second-guesses.

I was touched with a rush of emotion as I watched American teammates Phyllis Francis, Allyson Felix, and Natasha Hastings line up at the blocks for the finals. The world was wondering whether Bahaman Shaunae Miller would beat Allyson, who'd always been such a strong competitor and had dominated in the 200 for years. During the race, Shaunae seemed to pull ahead quickly, but Allyson powered forward, running her race with a strong, steady advance. In a dramatic finish, too close to call with the naked eye, Shaunae threw herself over the finish line, falling forward into the track. It was a finish few will forget. By the wonder of technology, officials decided that Shaunae's horizontal torso had crossed the finish line before Allyson's vertical one.

Watching that race was bittersweet. It felt strange offering my commentary on that photo finish when I would have loved to have been in the race.

At the same time, I was also loving what I was getting to do in the booth.

After I'd taken my final competitive steps at Hayward field, my "next step" had come knocking on my door when NBC invited me to broadcast with them. Today, I am loving the opportunities I'm being given to hone my skills as an on-camera journalist. It's exactly what I want to be doing.

Stepping Forward with Ross

If sports journalism was part of the natural progression for me as my cleats left the track, Ross and I are now also dipping our toes into other ventures that have developed naturally as a result of who we are and what we value.

I'll be the first person to admit that the life of an elite athlete is a necessarily self-centered way of living. Honestly, being a little self-focused is *required*. For me to perform at peak efficiency, I always had to give a lot of thought and attention to the foods I ate, the liquids I drank, the hours I slept, the work my body did. My dad wouldn't even let me carry my own bags up a flight of stairs! I'm aware that these luxuries aren't normal. I led a very unique and privileged existence. One that also included a lot of hard work!

But as a Christian, I've never lost sight of the fact that this life I've been given was never meant to be all about me. I believe we've been put on this earth to love others with God's love. While I built my professional track career, God gave me opportunities to love the people I was with. And now, both Ross and I are excited to pursue new opportunities to love others.

For years, he's been conducting free football clinics for kids. He does it because he's seen and experienced the value of athletics. He knows that when kids have access to sports, they begin to dream bigger dreams for their lives. In conjunction with education, those dreams can take them places they'd never reach otherwise. I've also been offering sports clinics across the United States to educate and empower young people with tools to excel on and off the track.

We both feel like we've received so much from our families and our communities, but we're very aware that there are so many children who don't have access to what we did. We're both passionate about raising money to help communities in need to flourish.

In both of our careers, we've known gifted young athletes who didn't have access to the resources required to train for elite competition. Fans don't always see the training, equipment, travel, and other expenses that are required to reach the highest levels of competition. Ross and I created a foundation together, called The Gold Standard Foundation, to support Olympic hopefuls whose dreams are limited by the cost of pursuing that goal.

I've also founded the Sanya Richards-Ross Fast Track Program. It is providing hundreds of children in Kingston, Jamaica, with literacy training, physical education, and healthy meals. Seven thousand kids who've been through the program are now reading at grade level. And they get to read a lot of books about sports that they love!

Closer to home, I've also recently launched a Girl Empowerment program in Central Texas to provide high school girls with leadership training. We do the same kind of vision boards together that I create to help me reach my goals! At the end of each program, our high-achievers receive a full makeover to attend their high school proms in style and confidence. We call it the Prom Glam!

It has been such a joy for both Ross and me to take what we've been given—great families, support from our communities, athletic talent, rich resources—and steward those in a way that allows others to flourish. We believe it's what our lives were meant for.

Sharing with Others

Though your path won't look just like mine, I do believe that you've been designed by God to thrive and also to use what you've been given to bless others. And it's beautiful to see the ways that God uses what we offer him with open hands.

In John's gospel, we get a peek behind the scenes at Jesus and his disciples before Jesus feeds five thousand people. His disciples are stumped about how they'll provide food for such a large crowd. Andrew offers, "Here is a boy with five small barley loaves and two small fish, but how far will they go among so many?" (John 6:9)

The answer, of course, is *not far*. But when that boy handed his lunch to Jesus, Jesus gave thanks to his Father and then distributed the meager offering, feeding the entire crowd.

When I was thirteen, I stood open-handed like that little boy. I gave God my heart and my body, and he did more than I could ever imagine.

Today, Ross and I are opening our hands to share from all we've been given.

And when you take what you've been given—the bread-and-fish lunch your mom packed for you, or your intelligence, or your love for those on the world's margins—Jesus can work with that.

Janelle is a writer. That's her day job. Over the last few years, Janelle has offered her pen, pencil, and keyboard to God. She helps high school students, who will be the first people in their family to attend college, write great essays for their college applications. She uses the skill God gave her.

Tanya loves growing vegetables. She is partnering with a ministry that serves people with and without disabilities. A lot of those folks struggle to find meaningful work. So Tanya is working with others to create a local urban farming business that can provide employment for people without work. She uses the passion God gave her.

Aliya speaks Arabic. Her church is building a friendship with a family that recently immigrated from Syria. The family has a twelve-year-old son who's struggling to learn English and do well in school. Twice a week, Aliya visits his house and helps him with his homework. She uses the gift God gave her.

I hope you're hearing what remarkable things God can do with the gifts he's given you. Whether that's engineering or pottery or sewing or mathematics, as you offer your gift—like the little boy with the lunch—God can bless others through you.

As you consider your next steps—whether that's choosing a college, deciding on a major, weighing grad school, or finding your first job—I want you to keep your hands open before God.

When you return to God what he's giving to you, there's nothing you can't accomplish.

RIGHT ON TRACK CHALLENGE

As long as you're on this earth, God has good work for you to do. What do you sense that you're being called to do next?

- Are you able to see which steps come next in your journey?
- Is there a natural progression from what you're doing right now?
- Is there something on the horizon that's completely new for you?
- Who's by your side to help you discern what's next?

Though none of us can see what the future holds, I'm confident there is good in store for you. What will help you keep a posture of openness for what God has next for you?

EPILOGUE

A s you think about running your race, one that's right on track for you, it's my hope and prayer that you heard two things.

First, I hope you heard that you were made for great things.

You have been fearfully and wonderfully made like no one else who's ever lived or ever will. You're valuable. You're precious. You're not here by chance. You've been designed to do something that no one else can do.

Maybe you'll string together words that no one else but you could write. Or you'll sing songs that only you can sing. Perhaps God will use your unique combination of intelligence and ingenuity in a laboratory, a classroom, a startup, or a television studio. Maybe God will use your unique capacity for love to serve the homeless, to lobby for justice in a courtroom, or to empower children to reach their own dreams. The possibilities of ways you will make your mark on God's world are endless. And although I can't begin to imagine the details of what living your unique calling will look like, I am certain you have been designed to live a life that is truly amazing and full.

Like me, you were made for great things.

Secondly, I want you to hear that success can never be measured by applause, endorsements, ribbons, or gold medals. Eventually, the applause grows dim. Endorsements end. Ribbons decay. Medals tarnish.

God inspired me to work hard and I'm incredibly grateful for all the opportunities I had. I wouldn't trade them for anything. And I'm proud of the way I ran my race—that I did it my way and with integrity. But while I'm grateful I won gold in London, I didn't need that win to validate who I am on the inside, who I am at my core. I didn't *need* that accolade to feel like a whole human being.

What makes me valuable and worthy, and what makes you valuable and worthy, is that we're children of God. I hope you can hear that as more than a cliché. Sometimes we're willing to believe that God loves the *world* (John 3:16) but we're less willing to believe that God loves *us*. God loves *me*. God loves *you*. God loves *you* so much that he sent his Son to die for you. That's big love. God loves *you* personally and knows every hair on your head. You are immeasurably precious to him.

When I think back on the best moments of my career, the applause and endorsements, the ribbons and medals weren't the things that mattered. What mattered was the coach who believed in me. What mattered was a family who walked beside me through thick and thin. What mattered was the moment I got to kiss Ross during my Olympic victory lap. What mattered were the *people*.

I hope you've had people in your life, as I did, who have been reflections of God's own love. But even if those folks were few and far between, you can still experience the reality of God's love as it flows through you to others. I believe that we have been put on this earth to serve others. And it's up to each one of us to figure out how that will look. You will find joy, peace, and satisfaction as you give yourself to loving others.

This past Sunday in church, my pastor said, "As a child of God, you're already living life from a place of victory."

Can you hear the good news in that? The *race* has already been won.

I can give you a tiny glimpse of what that's looked like for me. I went into the Games in London pretending like I'd already won. While that might sound crazy, it was actually pretty awesome. I was more joyful. I was less anxious. I was light and free. Doesn't that sound wonderful? That's what it means to live from a place of victory, and that's the gift we have in living as children of God. Christ has already won on our behalf. The results have been posted on the board and we share in his victory.

That changes everything.

When you run your race like you've already won, you can be more joyful. You can feel less anxious. You can walk through your unique, precious life as someone who's light and free. You don't get tripped up by small things because, at the end of the day, you're standing on the podium with your heavenly Father.

Living out your purpose in love, receiving God's love for you and sharing that love with others, is when you'll be truly happy and successful.

Live in victory,

Sanya

ACKNOWLEDGMENTS

God

I've always felt your presence and the tugging on my heart to share the good news with others. My first platform was on the track, using my talent and resolve as best I could to inspire. Now you've blessed me with this incredible opportunity to share my message through the pages of *Right on Track*. I've prayed throughout this entire process, I hope I've made you proud, and I pray this touches the lives of many.

Family & Loved Ones

Hubby: You are the greatest image of love and humility I have in my life. You teach me every day how to be a better person. You bring out the best in me. Thank you for always being in my corner and supporting me in everything I do. I stand tall because you prop me up. I love you . . . always and forever!

Dad: You're always there! It doesn't matter if the call comes at 1:00 a.m. or practice at 9:00 p.m. You're always ready and eager to help me fulfill my passions. No process feels complete without your stamp of approval or your encouraging words. Thanks for your willingness to help me make this book a reality.

Mom: Thanks for reading every page with me, for

jogging my memory and providing the supplements that no one else could! You have an ear and a heart that knows no bounds. This book is everything I wanted because of your guidance. I love you!

Shari: Even with your newborn son, you made time to listen to all my chapter ideas and attend my family book review sessions. You always make time for me and make space in your heart for my dreams. I love you and appreciate you more than you know.

Margot: You were so easy to work with. Thank you for making every effort to understand my goals for this book and making it come to life. I am so proud of the messages and the lessons we share in *Right on Track*. Your open heart and warm spirit made this experience unforgettable. Can't thank you enough.

My Team

To Carolyn, Jillian, Jacque, Marcus, and the entire Zondervan team, as well as David, Lowell, and Lis at CAA; thank you for believing in me and allowing me to publish this book! Love you guys so much!

DISCUSSION QUESTIONS FOR
RIGHT ON TRACK

1. Sanya explains how trying new things—even things she wasn't very good at—helped her build confidence and exercise courage. What are a few things you can try to stretch yourself to new limits? In what ways do fear, awkwardness, and insecurity hold you back?

2. How have Sanya's obstacles shaped her mindset today? Think about how you have dealt with obstacles like that in your life. How have these obstacles impacted your life in both the short term and long term?

3. "When I was nine, a setback propelled me to victory on the track. When I was twenty-nine, a setback propelled me to success off the track" (pg. 35). What is the difference between victory and success?

4. In what ways can you balance being you and being like the people you admire? How has Sanya accomplished this?

5. How does Sanya suggest facing changes that we choose? What about when changes choose us? What is the difference?

6. Sanya's faith is the anchor that centers her in the ways that matter most. What identities define you?

7. What strategies does Sanya suggest to rise above negativity? In the face of defeat or challenges, how can you remind yourself to hold your head high and walk with dignity?

8. Think of the people who are in your cheering section. In what ways have these people impacted your life's journey? How can you cheer these people on?

9. Sanya encourages you to take a victory lap—to relish your own successes. What milestones in your life can you celebrate?

10. What gifts have you been given that you can use to help others flourish?